HOW TO BE A PROPERTY MANAGER

South of France

Author: Gill Meredith

INDEX

Appendices
Business Tools and Documents

A. Example of a Kbis
B. Client contract
C. Keyholder contract
D. Example of a task sheet and cash float management
E. Managing fire, flood and theft
F. Introductory email to assess a house for rental
G. Costs to rent your home
H. Property rental checklist
 I. Rental contract
 J. A-Z house folder
 K. Seasonal additions to house checks

INTRODUCTION

The role of a Property Manager is a varied one. It can be managing holiday homes in various parts of the world; the management and administration of a collection of properties in a development or simply helping out a neighbour with a weekend holiday home next door.   The person fitting the role could be someone operating a business with a high degree of responsibility through to a neighbour holding a key purely in case of emergencies.

This guide is aimed at the former and my role as a Property Manager looking after holiday homes in the South of France. If you are thinking of working for yourself and in France then this guide will be of help even if you are thinking of a different role. If you want to be a Property Manager in a different country then I am confident there will still be valuable advice and information despite the different nationality, culture and environment.

There are tips on handling bureaucrats, how to create a business, the day to day role and how to close a business. Many of the holiday homes were rented out as a source of income and details are provided on how to manage rentals and the associated documentation. I was often contacted about selling one of my client's homes or helping tourists to buy a home so reference is also made to this function.

You will find a wide selection of real stories that occurred at the many properties and these are interspersed with practical advice.

The Property Manager wears many hats!

CHAPTER 1
Cultural Differences

I imagine anyone changing the location from their country of birth to living and working abroad, must have already decided that they like the country and have an adequate command of the language. This was the case for me whilst also appreciating that not everyone was in love with France or the French. The British and French have always had a love/hate relationship and I suspect our close physical proximity has meant many of my compatriots confuse proximity with assuming they must know the French who some have decided are rude or arrogant. You only have to look at the cultural differences within Europe to realise that proximity is not to be confused with a need to understand the history of a country and its people before you have the right to criticise and to judge.

Having visited many parts of Asia, the smiling face is all encompassing. It's their default face whether you smile first and create the reaction or if they just offer it up without any provocation. In France it is not the same, their default is not a smile – not even a grin. They have plenty of them but they are habitually kept for family and close friends; a stranger arriving at a French airport or train station should have no reason to expect a beaming smile welcoming the person to their country – they are more likely to interpret your own smile as suspicious or showing superiority. I have occasionally been successful eliciting a smile from a complete stranger, however, it has often been via a clever play of words in French or schmoozing a male civil servant with a coy play of femininity. I hate it but, subject to what you want to achieve, then you have to adopt whatever is required to obtain the end result.

It also helps to engage the person in a pre-amble of what you want to achieve rather than by-passing this to the details of what you need them to do. They will probably just tell you all the reasons why they can't help so do not underestimate getting them on side. What might be "absolutely impossible" at the beginning can easily turn into "I'll see what I can do" if only approached the right way and taking into account the ciphered code of conduct that is fundamentally the French way. When dealing with civil servants, although it can be incredibly time-consuming and frustrating, it is always a good tip to take the time to explain what you want to achieve and inveigle their support; coax, manoeuver, cajole or whatever it takes rather than jump in with two feet before setting out your table of needs. For the most part, the French will go the extra mile when you need it but how you approach getting their help will collapse at the first hurdle if you do not approach it in a manner they recognise as bien élevé (well brought up and well educated).

It's a secret language which, if you don't learn how to translate it, then you will forever feel affronted by French people who you will continue to perceive as rude and dismissive. For their part, the French can often interpret foreigners' actions as impolite, aggressive and bizarre.

One of the areas that I noted and corrected early on was my ability to ask someone a question such as "where will I find …… ?" without any front end pleasantry even if I was in a hurry or I deemed it unnecessary. This is incredibly rude to a French person and immediately declares that you are a foreigner. The minimum should be a "Bonjour Madame" or "Bonjour Monsieur" or even better after the obligatory two word introduction to add "Excusez moi de vous déranger mais j'ai besoin de/je cherche …...." *(sorry to disturb you but I need/I am looking for ……)*. No matter how much of a hurry you are in, you will be perceived as ignorant to seek help before introducing the minimum courtesy – even if you are ringing to report a fire in your house and the flames are licking at your heels!

Many foreigners visiting or living in France have learned the minefield that is "you" which can either be the familiar "tu" or the polite "vous". Many of the young have adopted a much more relaxed style of speaking and use "tu" even if they don't know you even though this is deemed as mal élevé (badly brought up as a child and badly educated). The use of "tu" is never to be encouraged and do not get lulled into a false practice. Always use "vous" when talking to anyone and most certainly when speaking to elderly people. If someone is happy for you to "tutoyer" them (the verb noting to use tu) they will tell you, however, until they say "tu peux me tutoyer" (*you can use tu*) then absolutely stay within the confines of "vous". This is true even if you think you have a great relationship with a work colleague or a workman, continue to use "vous" and wait for them to offer up the use of "tu" in your relationship.

When I first came to France, I joined a small team that put together the quarterly village newsletter. I thought it would help with my integration. I had come from an English office and had worked for many British and American companies. I was used to the structured meetings with a set of topics to discuss and actions to agree. I was not ready for what greeted me. The first horror was the late arrival of many of the participants. In the U.K., a late arriver would make their excuses, slide into their chair and make a point of catching someone on the way out to find out what they had missed. Not here in France where no apology was made and the meeting was regurgitated to the point of the latecomer's arrival. This would carry on as each latecomer made their entrance. It's a wonder anything got done but then that it in itself presented a problem. There was plenty of involvement and discussion on every subject but no clear instruction or action ever seemed to result. I had witnessed this when I worked in Paris but there I had the benefit of a British boss also on secondment. It was only when I was not in a meeting that he chaired that the lengthy roundabout discussions would prevail as I was seen as in the minority.

This also highlights that the French have a respect for hierarchical roles in companies. They work well with peers and see any manager or director above them as to be treated with respect even if they arrive late to their meetings. It's all about rank, where you fit and also how well you have been brought up and educated. Like many countries, France seems to operate on a "who you know" basis and the relationships that you have created. It's all part of their history of where you sit within the class structure. Writing or speaking can be a clear indicator of where you are within this order. This can equate to their level of motivation to help you. When you arrive as a visitor, or to live in their country, it is no wonder that you present confusion to them as they have nothing to gauge you on. Added to that, if you stomp over their language badly expressing yourself, it is not that surprising that the blank face that you perceive has no warmth and is potentially rude, is just the person hastily trying to calculate who they have in front of them.

Another area that can cause foreigners to scratch their heads and bitterly complain is the inability of the French to admit failure or blame. To admit either of these is to be avoided at all cost and everyone understands this from a young age. As a Property Manager, I have had many reasons to complain to EDF (electricity supplier) Orange (one of the many phone and internet suppliers), or SAUR (water supplier). You could explain the most appalling service and problems but you could never expect any form of apology or accountability. They will listen and will tell you what they will do about it but the default is never to lay blame or to apologise. That is a really tough learning curve if you have worked in other countries with a very different interpretation of "customer service".

I once worked for a Japanese company and I think there are many similarities in as much as people will not blame their company or colleagues for poor service and they also adopted a style of meeting that was all about discussion and consensus on future actions. Few managers dictated what would be done, they coerced their teams to see the reason why it was the appropriate action. If anyone was against a decision, they would use a technique called *clipboard management* where they had small one-on-one discussions until sufficient numbers of people were "on side" for whatever action was required. I see this operating in a similar way in France.

It would be extremely hard to be a Property Manager in France if your French is basic. When I first moved to France in 2003, I had a decent command of the language as I had used it either on holiday or when working in France. It was by no means fluent and it did not need to be, however, I could explain a missing word of vocabulary by elaborating on the subject until the French person supplied the word that I did not know.

I have never known any other country as proud of their language as the French. They ensure their children write and speak to an extremely high standard and this is part of the problem when they opt not to speak to you in English even if they understand what you are saying. You know they can speak it as they've uttered a word or two, however, unless they can communicate without any errors whatsoever then they will not speak in English as they fear making mistakes and this will be totally unacceptable to them. Most of the French remember their English lessons from school so appreciate "la plume de ma tante" or their equivalent "Johnny is in the kitchen" is not high on the list of useful vocabulary. They are hugely appreciative when you make the effort to communicate with them in their language, they are very forgiving of errors and are very encouraging. I have been corrected mid-sentence a handful of times but those occasions are extremely rare and I encourage people to give it a go and you will certainly see that all elusive smile as they recognise the attempts you are making that they would never make in return in your language.

The love of their language starts very early and is drummed into them from primary school and continues right through to higher education. How you speak and how you write is one of the main determinators of your class and rank. It is no surprise that French street names herald from their history and their famous authors and poets. Every town or village seems to have a Rue Frédéric Mistral or an Avenue Victor Hugo as the country pays homage to its great writers and honours its language and its history.

Beware of the false translation or the *franglais* which is bound to emit laughter and squeals of delight. Some words in English do not translate into the same meaning in French such as "sensible" which means "sensitive" or "responsive". They would use "raisonnable" to describe a sensible person. Many words in French can have several meanings and sometimes this can be the reason behind the expressionless face as they struggle to understand or to adjust an English word that's been offered up with a completely different meaning for them. I learned early on to use the verb avoir (have) when talking of body temperature so "I am hot" would be "J'ai chaud" and most definitely not "Je suis chaud" which would imply you are keen to get your clothes off with the person in front of you and have a bit of sexual interaction! Even though this pitfall was noted and avoided, I still fell into a trap when talking to the elderly mother of a builder when I first arrived in France. I had phoned their home to ask if the builder could quote to redo the cement floor of my courtyard. In my confusion I asked the poor woman if she could ask her son to come and "faire le cour" (which I thought was *to do the courtyard*). I had just asked the elderly mother if she could send her son over to make love to me!

There are many pitfalls and it's surprising how many words that you think translate directly from English to French take on a completely different meaning and they often have a sexual connotation! I have seen some odd French to English translations as well so it is not a one-way situation. A particular favourite of mine is on menus where the translations can be hugely entertaining. I once read *Crottin de chèvre chaud* that had been translated as "hot goat dung" when in fact it's a type of small, round goat's cheese!

It is interesting to note that the French do not cut corners when writing in their language. Something written precisely in English, which might take a line on a page of paper, can quite easily become two lines or more to express the same thing in French. They love their language and they do not abbreviate or eliminate words just for the sake of brevity. Other than children and young adults, they remain extremely upset by the introduction of English and American words into their everyday language even if they have no equivalent word.

I learned fairly early on that written Business French is extremely difficult and most letters that I send, even with a decent level of language ability, undoubtedly scream "Spot The Brit" to the patient French who must wince and snarl at every clumsy grammatical error or poor use of syntax.

One of the noticeable differences when living in France is their very different relationship with money. In the U.K, and if you are working, it is feasible to apply for a mortgage or you can live a life on credit if you so wish. France is very nervous of granting mortgages which results in so many early twenty year olds still living with parents and the French live much more within their means, having a healthy respect for what they can afford. This level of fiscal control means that it is extremely serious to write a cheque knowing that insufficient funds are in the account. The banks permit this two or three times and then they close the account and you are unable to get a bank account in France for three years which I imagine must be incredibly difficult in the day-to-day running of your life.

I recommend reading a little about French etiquette if you are embarking on a trip to France. It is incredibly easy to cause offence through the most well-meant of gestures. This could be through discussion at the dinner table or the type of gift given to a host or maybe talking in detail about your money or voting preferences (both of which are strict taboos). If you do not have local help and guidance, you can walk clumsily in hobnail boots over people's sensitivities and there's a limit to the amount of times perceived bad manners can be put down as "cultural differences". You are the foreigner abroad and France has the right to insist that you learn and adapt rather than compare and contrast.

CHAPTER 2
The Background and Business Decision

I think it was no surprise to my family that I would eventually move to France. It was a part of the world where I always felt more alive and I loved the French language: the structure, the musicality, the sexiness. Many moons ago, I recall my teacher advising me not to embark on the "A" level examination as I would not succeed and yet here I am living in the country with a very decent command of French proving that it is good to listen to your inner voice.

My love of the language was hugely helped by having a French correspondent. I guess this might not be so fashionable now but it was instrumental in laying down a good foundation of the language. My pen pal lived in Angers in the Maine and Loire region and there is no doubt that the fortnightly holidays immersed in family life were conducive to my love of the country. It was also a good introduction to the speed at which people could speak and also the varied dialects. I was a sponge soaking up the everyday slang and expressions that brought the language alive rather than the school textbooks which were so dry and stilted.

Prior to my move to the country, I had a brief foray working for three months in Paris. Before that and when I was between jobs, I stayed a couple of months in Provence, in the South, wondering if the time was right to work and live in the area. I had used the language off and on for holidays and business which is key to any language otherwise it's definitely a case of "use it or lose it". If you want to be a Property Manager you will definitely need to speak the language of the country. For example, even if you are an English speaker and perhaps living in the Dordogne region of France, which is much beloved by the British, you will still need to speak French to communicate with all the utility companies, the artisans, the bureaucrats. There is no way around it. You will need to speak French.

As it transpired it would be another nine years after my stay in Provence before I eventually made the move here as all my ducks were in a row to make it happen, or the stars were aligned, or whatever turn of phrase you wish. When I think back, the appeal was always there but the circumstances were just not right and you need both. I was not married and I did not have children therefore the decision, though life-changing, would only affect me and it was a risk that I could take.

After I moved into my home near Avignon, it was not long before I was contacted by the estate agent who sold me my house. She wanted to know if I would work for her and her husband. Most agents are paid a commission from a sale and are not salaried. It is the norm. I agreed on the basis that they would help with some of the costs. I did a lot of driving around but not much came of it and I left them before my lack of income could present a problem. It was only when

I met a couple on a flight to the U.K. that I saw the potential of Property Management.

The couple had just made another trip to see about six properties that all failed their check list owing to lack of attention by the estate agent. They were looking to move to France and were in search of a permanent home. I suggested they could pay me to go and see the properties first and produce a report on suitability rather than them having to book a flight, book a hire car, book a hotel, eat out every night, etc. I liaised with the estate agents and saw the properties they selected via the internet. This ultimately resulted in them buying a 19th century stone house and they asked if I could help them manage the restoration as their French was very limited and they were not used to the speed at which the people in the South could speak or the Provencal twang that distorted textbook French that we'd all learned. At the same time as attending the meetings that we had with builders, electricians and plumbers, I also thought about the wider picture and how to get more clients and make Property Management an actual business.

I created computer-produced marketing flyers of my Property Management business in English and French – nothing fancy just a Word document with a border - and I placed them under the windscreen wipers of any car in the surrounding area with a foreign number plate. I also delivered a few around my village. I produced about 250 and I had none left at the end of the week. I immediately had four hits resulting in potential work. I decided to pursue this route and work for myself but I was totally unclear of the next step other than meeting the house owners.

Working "undeclared" in France would not fit with my character and even the French only abuse the system occasionally so I "Googled" what to do to start a business and this led me some months later to a meeting with the Chamber of Commerce in the pretty village of Beaucaire.   Fifteen years later I can still recall the meeting and the advisor.   It was the first brick in building my business.

CHAPTER 3
Creating the Business

So with just a little or maybe a lot of appreciation in understanding the cultural differences, what does it take to launch your business? The first thing that presents a head-scratching "What? Are you having a laugh?" moment is establishing the type of business. France is suffocating under different business models from the Micro-Entreprise to SARL, EI, SA, EURL, SAS, SCI and more. As if there were not enough already, in 2009 Nicolas Sarkozy, who at least acknowledged some of the small business issues, introduced yet another totally new system called Auto-Entrepreneur. This was a viable green light to the young French who were moving abroad in significant numbers to find other countries where it was easier to start a business and it was also to keep the many small businesses in France from folding and closing their doors. As a child, I grew up recognising that France had a huge infrastructure of small businesses and self-employed workers (*travailleurs indépendants*) – the local electrician, plumber and small independent shopkeepers in the High Street.

The protests of "Gilets Jaunes" in 2018, which flashed across newspapers and television screens, actually started life as the artisans trying to keep their small businesses functioning and the citizens kicking back from increased taxes introduced too fast by Macron and attempted during the presidency of François Hollande. Unfortunately, the damage caused by the "gilets jaunes" extremists broke the true spirit of the French people as they saw their historical monuments graffitied and destroyed. A true French person holds these treasures of their history very dear. Mess with them at your peril.

But back to the Chamber of Commerce at Beaucaire where I had decided to wait a little while before arranging the appointment as I needed to get a better feel of whether I could grow my small number of clients. At the meeting I talked through the type of business that I wanted to start. Even the nature of what I wanted to do created a *"Computer Says No!"* scenario as the nature of my work did not fit any of the listed businesses in the software options. I did not realise at the time that it was a role that would surprisingly scratch heads in many bureaucratic organisations.

I opted for "Micro-Entreprise Simplifiée" which meant that I paid tax on only 50% of my income which was not an insignificant decision. I never paid tax on my business earnings up to closing the business, however, I got no other benefits. I could not offset my petrol expenses nor could I claim part of my house being used as an office, etc. I also had to pay an annual fee called "Cotisation Foncière des Entreprises", known as the CFE, which was around 400 euros and is based on your reported income. I believe I chose the right option, however, it was a key question at the start and my understanding was helped by meeting a very friendly and receptive advisor at the Chamber of Commerce. Since that meeting I have met many officials who have not been as friendly or open in communication as this particular lady.

The biggest tip that I can give you when starting a business here in France is the unasked question that holds a multitude of potential changes to your decision. The French are extremely good at answering the question but they answer it and it stops right there; no illumination, no "but be careful of this" or "you could also do this". Any official is usually cut from the same cloth; the banks, the administrators, the police, etc. They answer the question that you have asked them. It is not their job to think of what that means to you or of the other questions that might arise based on their reply. It's up to you to interpret their reply and pose any other questions it could spawn and, therefore, up to you to ask those questions that could ultimately make you change your mind.

You need to think on your feet to ensure all your queries are answered before the door is firmly shut. I touch on that point in the cultural variances as, in fairness to the French, you have asked a question and they have answered it. The approach is certainly to feel free to ask another question, however, I am not paid to anticipate or define the questions that you might need to ask me. When dealing with the bureaucrats in later years, I operated much more like them. A brief reply. No elaboration unless I was asked another question. I can definitely see the merits!

So, once we overcame the computer software glitches that couldn't find my type of business, we decided that looking after holiday homes fell under the title of "Services de Prestations". I explained that I would be checking over houses to ensure all was OK inside and outside. Dear Lord, I had no idea how wide that brief would get sometimes! I used the word "contrôle" in speaking to her. Interestingly, she put particular emphasis on the fact that I must not put that word on any marketing or advertising as "contrôle des maisons" was more aligned to security companies and security staff even though the word is noted on my Kbis (document noting the creation of the business). I was happy to take her advice as I realised that I could not afford business insurance once I understood the costs involved of starting my company. I was starting up very much as a small operator and any early unnecessary costs were subject to my questioning scrutiny!

Whilst discussing some of the functions that I would be doing, which helped her identify the business category, I did not really appreciate that she would take some of my descriptions and add them to the business under the title of "Services des Prestations". If you look at the example of the Kbis (in the Appendix) you will see rather a brief and arbitrary list. If I had known that this information was to be documented, I would have been more prepared and ensured a more comprehensive list was supplied.

After only a few years I noted that I was being strangled by the Micro-Entreprise business subscriptions (the French equivalent of National Insurance). After the Auto entrepreneur system was implemented, I thought a change of business type would make sense. Yet again, nothing is that simple as an accountant explained I could only change my existing system for a maximum of three years before returning back to Micro-Entreprise. It would also significantly hit my pension contributions. His advice was to not change and to never earn more than 14,000 euros per year followed by a very expressive and exaggerated wink! Now the auto-entrepreneur model no longer exists as it has been amalgamated into Micro-Entreprise. It's a can of worms and you really need to give significant thought to the benefits of each type of business model – particularly if you are recruiting personnel.

One of the frustrations of running a business in France is the cost to grow your business by employing staff. There is a crazy system whereby you pay an employee a salary but then you have to commit to a further huge percentage of that amount in payments to the state to cover N.I. contributions, etc. Make sure you understand each type of structure and get professional help, such as the Chambre des Commerce (for sales) or the Chambre de Metier (for artisans), before committing to the structure that will affect the amount of your monthly business contributions. Do not assume your business is "commerçant" or "metier" as, naturally, it is not always obvious.

Another difficulty of my new business was that I could not estimate my income as I did not know how many clients I would get. Without this, there was an enforced minimum charge for year 1 which was immediately payable in full (this payment being the equivalent of the UK's national insurance system). Year 2 was also payable up front at the beginning of the year. Only at Year 3 would there be sufficient history from the two previous years for the income charges to be estimated and become payable via monthly direct debit. Another thing to note was that there were minimum platforms of payment irrespective of your income so, for example, I would have to pay a minimum percentage per month into the "maternité" (*state maternity*) charges. This was one of the reasons the accountant told me not to earn more than 14,000 euros in order that my subscriptions stayed at the minimum of each platform. It was tough that I had to pay out 2600 euros immediately to start the first year of my business. This was one of the deterrents for young French entrepreneurs and why they often went abroad to get a foothold on their business idea as the cost to try out an idea was significantly less than it was in France. Now, that system has changed and not before time. Businesses can be set up and are based on "a no income = no charge" in the first year although you clearly need to set funds aside for the charges which will eventually become payable once your first year has been completed and if you have earned money.

CHAPTER 4
Early Clients

With the four potential clients lined up, meetings held and attended, I embarked on working for myself. I had been told that I had to create invoices with a strict set of wording to acknowledge that my invoices were not eligible for tax based on a "start up" scenario and within the micro business model. Fortunately, I did not need to wait for the full registration documentation to arrive as that followed many weeks later. I just had to commit to a start date and payment.

Some weeks after the Beaucaire meeting, I received paperwork confirming my business together with a copy of my Kbis. This is a document that confirms the legal entity of the business and confirms the details of the owner, date of inscription, etc. A covering lettering confirmed that I would be issued a SIREN number in the following weeks (a unique French business identification number).

Considerable thought was given to how much I wanted to charge for my services. There were a number of large companies with flashy web sites who operated a house management service aimed at holiday homes. They requested owners sign an annual contract with them with a minimum fee that did not take into account any additional services other than house/garden surveillance. I wanted to set myself apart from them and I felt that annual contracts could be unattractive and costly. I preferred working with an hourly rate and an additional charge for mileage. As some jobs could take just fifteen minutes (e.g. watering a courtyard), I was loathe to charge a full hour so I often charged smaller amounts by putting myself in the position of the client and assuming what might be acceptable.

The one note of caution that I would suggest when setting an hourly rate is to ensure it is not too low. Over time, the clients became my friends and these friendships could make it difficult when increasing my prices. This was not because they would complain at an increase but more the uncomfortable feeling that a price increase generated within me. I tended to operate on the hourly rate irrespective of the task, therefore, it could be very manual, such as doing a house check, ranging through to consultancy on house sales. After a few years, I decided to split out certain tasks that I deemed as a more expensive service – such as house rental consultancy. It was helpful to charge for mileage as I had a handful of clients that were up to an hour's drive from my home. I did not want to inflate my base hourly rate to accommodate these clients so it was easier to set a mileage fee and based on parameters such as 10 to 30 kilometres and increasing upwards.

At that time, I would take any client just to help develop the business even though I could sense that some of the people (or their houses) were a potential risk. I became aware that most of the holiday home business near my area was wrapped up by either an

English husband and wife team or a single lady. The latter seemed to be everywhere and well known by all the holiday home clientele. She appeared to only operate in cash and, after many years, just disappeared. Did those in the Trésor (*Tax Office*), who must have turned a blind eye for so long, just get too close?

Ninety percent of my client base turned into good friends and we would often share a glass of rosé or three when they visited their houses. One of the reasons that I think helped create the friendships was a clear demarcation between work and pleasure. I heard stories of property managers visiting their clients and discussing new projects and house issues and then enjoying a drink that could extend for several hours. They billed the whole time they were with them! Certainly, the business and friendship roles could merge but it was clearly a choice to invoice a fair amount for the business side of discussions versus a lunchtime or evening aperitif spanning a number of hours.

Those early days involved a small handful of clients; some in or near my village and some in nearby towns. I helped the original British couple purchase their house and then continued with them to project manage the restorations. Their level of French could not cope with the challenging local accent. I had already grasped the provencale une verre du "ving" rather than the expected "vin" (*a glass of wine*) and "c'est bing" rather than "c'est bien" (*that's great*).

It was all valuable experience and my vocabulary was starting to expand from everyday pleasantries to the intricacies of crumbling drains, leaky roofs and installing parafoudres (surge protectors) in fuse boxes. This vocabulary was learned over time or researched before a meeting so it was not something that I knew before I became a Property Manager.

CHAPTER 5
Marketing, Contracts, Invoicing and Tax

Naturally, with a new business, thought needed to be given to future marketing. I created a web site with "Vistaprint" using a software that was clunky and not particularly user friendly. I used them again years later and it had undergone a radical improvement. I also created one with "Godaddy" and I have to say their site and templates were more modern and easier to build. "Vistaprint" remain extremely useful as they do not just offer building a web site, they offer all the tools that you might need such as business cards, clothing, stickers for cars, flyers pamphlets, etc. This ensures that you have one look and image for the business which is hard to replicate with just a web site supplier unless you want to pay copyright costs to use templates.

My web site was mostly just a place to point people to. It occasionally brought enquiries or new business and directing people to read it was a speedy solution. It covered an example of tasks within the property management role, reference to project management of restorations, photos and links to property rentals and my contact details and hourly rates. Over time, I added a French translation of the text. After the four clients that I acquired from leaving pamphlets on the cars with foreign number plates, plus the web site, I never had to advertise or produce any further marketing materials. Word of mouth proved to be the biggest influencer in growing my client base. This was understandable given that I would be holding house keys and usually had free rein of a property. Naturally, people wanted to talk to their friends about my character and ability before asking to meet me. This meant that I also never used social media in promoting my services. I have never been a fan of Facebook, Instagram and other Twitty speak stuff. These tools seem to attract more Spam than be of great commercial use but I am certain that this is owing to my lack of acumen in using them properly and they are clearly the way forward. When developing a business, you need any tools at your disposal so they are not to be dismissed even though Property Managers often work via recommendation.

An unexpected and simple marketing tool came in the use of clothing. I would ruin my own clothes during the long hot summers owing to the constant washing and ironing. I decided to get some polo shirts via Vistaprint. On the front, I indicated my name, Property Management, and my mobile phone number. I acquired a good handful of clients through just wearing these polo shirts and being stuck in a queue at a supermarket. My name could not be construed as a French name so the conversation always started in English and along the lines of "do you look after holiday homes? We're looking for someone to ………". Do not underestimate the value of having your name and phone number across your left boob!

The pamphlet drop on foreign cars and through foreign named letterboxes would often result in people contacting me many months later; two different clients even contacted me years later. It was the sort of role that a holiday home owner would get the flyer and pop in a drawer in case something was required later on. I had a surprising number of people who came via that route. It was also not unknown for me to follow an English voice and introduce my services. When you work for yourself you have to have a certain amount of chutzpah.

Managing the business workload could be very challenging. Some days were full on and could be affected by the time of the year. Understandably the winter months were always calmer as fewer owners were using their homes and the winter months were a time of recuperation for me after the madness of the summer and the additional business from house rentals. As mentioned, the exorbitant state charges to take on staff was a huge deterrent and it kept me from growing the business owing to the limited number of clients that I could manage on my own. The alternative was to offer part-time work but this was nigh on impossible to implement. A typical week would be manageable for me, however, in July or August, I would long for the odd hour or two of support. This could not be guaranteed from one day to the next and it made it impossible to interest anybody. No firm commitment of hours and, therefore, no firm commitment of payment. It was a stranglehold that made me turn away clients from time to time - a concept so alien to my years in business in the U.K. I drew on my sister, who lived in England, to help me occasionally and she would always keep a week or two clear for a visit in the tourist high season.

It is useful to explain a bit about how I invoiced for my work as this is a job that can have a gap of many months before you see the holiday home owners again. Each duty could have a very low value in terms of invoicing but all of these visits would add up and so I got into the habit of always adding any client activity at the end of the working day and before I forgot to record a visit that could be one of six or more ranging from a few minutes to a few hours. In the Appendix you will see how I captured the activity per client which was duly noted on an Excel task diary to be invoiced later on. I usually invoiced once I'd reached around 150 euros just to ensure funds were arriving regularly enough to pay the monthly direct debit for the business subscriptions. Most clients paid almost immediately or within three weeks. I would also ask for a cash float when I saw them as there were always purchases to be made unless it was working for someone who lived in France full-time. It would typically be used for swimming pool chlorine tablets, damp course replacement tablets, ant powder, wasp killer, etc. I controlled the cash float and kept all the invoices or receipts for any purchases. It was also not unknown for the occasional artisan to insist on cash.

It had been explained back in the days of the Beaucaire meeting with the Chamber of Commerce that it was best to keep income separate from purchases otherwise an invoice total could be deemed as revenue and would be taxable. I, therefore, insisted on a cash float and ensured I always kept the original receipts in case of a tax audit. I gave photocopies to the clients. I emailed tax invoices on letterhead paper together with the Excel task list; these lists provided the date and the detailed information per task. The invoices had to have "TVA non applicable, article 293 B du CGI" added to them as one of the requirements of the Micro-Entreprise business structure. The Excel sheet explaining what I did in detail was extremely popular as clients felt more closely aligned to what I was doing when I went to their house. Years later, I tried to remove the Excel sheet to reduce costs but nobody wanted to forego the detail and preferred me to keep it as part of the invoicing process.

During my business years, apart from the one visit to an accountant to identify the benefits of the recently introduced Auto-Entrepreneur business system, I never used an accounting service and I did all my own Tax Declarations. As I was not able to offset any expenses, it was not a complex form to complete. The hardest part of the annual tax form was identifying which of the many boxes covered "Service de Prestations" as the form was split between artisans and commerçants of which I was the latter. In the early days, I would go to the local Tax Office, take a ticket in the Waiting Room (like the system to wait your turn at a supermarket) and eventually get a face to face meeting with someone who could answer any questions. Nowadays, you book a telephone call on line so it is a much more efficient and convenient system. I always wondered if I would get a tax audit but one never materialised. I was recording income of around 14,000 euros or less so I suppose the Trésor had much bigger fish to fry and the sprats were left to swim freely.

For the most part, I drew up client contracts although I have to confess that in the early days I did not always have these in place and, having become close friends with the clients, it seemed uncomfortable to then ask them to sign a formal agreement. Once the number of clients increased, I realised that I needed to cover my arse! I had a mini contract that just charged a nominal fee to act as a key holder and I had one or two of these contracts. The owners had informed the village or town Mairie (*Town Hall*) that I held a key for emergencies such as flood, fire, or theft. I drew up a larger, and much more comprehensive, contract covering the selection of services that were available for other roles (see Appendix).

A benefit that sits well within this chapter is to confirm the merits of having a SIREN number. For most of my working life I either had company cars or benefited from using cars on long term rental. This method was ideal during the working years. The long term rental contracts usually lasted 3 years and, just before the contract expiry date, I would be contacted to either buy the existing car which was never a realistic option, commit to a new vehicle, or to end the contract.

In France there was a similar system and I used the contracts the same way so I rarely had huge bills other than maintenance servicing and a couple of replacement front tyres.   It was comforting to know that the car was unlikely to breakdown; particularly being a single woman and always driving alone. In the years before I closed my business, I think I must have had a second sense that I wanted a change as I decided to purchase a new car rather than taking out another rental contract. Having my SIREN number permitted a 17% reduction in the price of a new car so considerable savings were to be made. I ended up negotiating a further few percent so drove away with a 22% discount on the price and owning my own car for the first time in many years.

Now that I look back at that decision, I realise it was one of my better ones. There's quite a few in the other pile!

CHAPTER 6
Clients: The Good, the Bad, and the Downright Ugly!

It is with a sense of pride that I realise that every client meeting produced work; apart from one local villager who took all my rental knowledge but then managed rentals himself. Apart from him, everyone thanked me for my time and signed on the dotted line. Part of that success was due to the level of preparation when attending a meeting. I would have a folder in French and a folder in English. Inside, I would have draft contracts, a wide range of rental data, my charges, and a small biography in French from our village newspaper. I had multiple copies so that I could leave examples where necessary and I was prepared with contracts if one could be signed. Some of the rental data was too sensitive to leave as it was a potential money-earner in offering a level of consultancy so think carefully about any documentation you leave with a prospect.

Within a short period of time I was becoming very informed about holiday homes. There were many areas, including house insurance, where few owners had noted the specifics regarding properties left empty for more than fourteen days (some variations on length of time exist). The owners had an obligation to ensure all water supplies were cut off and also electricity and gas where stipulated. Few actually did this and I knew that this would mean, in the event of any claim, that only a portion of any repair costs would be met. Another insurance stipulation could be for chimneys to be swept on an annual basis. For more regular visitors, I learned when to turn off water tanks to be more cost effective rather than leaving them switched on – a price break that is normally around an absence of eight weeks. All this information was gathered incrementally with each additional house and type of property (new build, villa or the old stone houses originating from 19th century or earlier). The latter were always charming and full of character, however, it was no surprise that the French far preferred the modern, new builds with air-conditioning and less maintenance. In all my time in France, I haven't yet seen one of the stone houses without some area of damp and to varying degrees of impact. My own house included.

I think my confidence was reassuring for home owners who felt their house was in a "safe pair of hands". For my part, I treated each one as if it was my own so I was braced for sleepless nights as and when problems occurred with one of my charges.

Home owners often had a key with a neighbour and called upon them from time to time but many of these clients felt that they needed a more regular intervention and didn't want to put upon their Gallic friends. I appreciated that neighbours could be hugely useful but I also understood that the owners didn't want to push these punctuated friendships too far. It was important to be sensitive to the neighbours so that I did not appear as the English woman taking charge over something which was a bond between them and their neighbours. It's also true that the French have an aversion to being accountable to the extent they will often feel nervous of holding keys. A break-in can cause a gendarme or an insurance assessor to question a key-holding neighbour and, as with all insurance agents, they actively seek out someone else to blame and to pay costs!

One of the early clients were another British couple who had purchased a large house in a nearby mediaeval town but they spoke no French. I worked for quite a long time with them as they installed a new kitchen, rewired, painted the interior, and constructed a swimming pool. They had suffered bankruptcy status before their purchase. I assume, owing to this, wherever possible they wanted to pay cash to pay a reduced bill. This came back to bite them when they came to sell the house as the majority of the work could not be offset on capital gains tax charges as they had no invoices. Those buying a holiday home in France can offset improvements against the difference between their purchase price and the eventual sales price but only on production of supporting invoices. For example, my first clients, who eventually sold their house, spent at least 15,000 euros on a new kitchen yet they could not offset any of their bills as a kitchen already existed in the house at the time of purchase; even though all it had was a free-standing stove, a sink and no kitchen units whatsoever.

The property checks and arising issues formed the majority of my work, however, not everything that I did sat fully within "Services de Prestations". I was not about to open another business model with more business charges just to accommodate the French system so a degree of creativity was necessary. Naturally, I would not embark on something outside of the obvious remit unless I had full approval from the client and I had to tread carefully working with estate agents when helping clients buy or sell houses as I was not registered as an agent.

There were many other hats that I wore that did not fit that easily with Property Management but it gave me a chance to do many crazy things such as investigating how a British man could arrange a PACS agreement (civil union agreement) in France with his Brazilian boyfriend. It appeared France was more lenient on the visa complications than the U.K. Another time I spent a number of weekends roaming a local market searching for some Ecuadorian pan pipe players that someone wanted to book for a summer party. The client actually wanted to book a superb jazz trio who were regularly at the market but I remember asking their price which I relayed back and then was put on a mission to find the pan pipe players who would have, undoubtedly, been cheaper ……… had I found them!

Other more bizarre roles included rescuing a cat stuck up a 25m cypress tree which involved me hanging out of a window with a net, then another time picking the olives off three trees in the garden of a Swedish couple and getting them converted into olive oil at the local mill. A period when I learnt that they have to be put in plastic crates and not cardboard boxes and that they can be attacked by worms if left too long on the tree. I also got involved with the Trésor (*Treasury*) trying to resolve a business issue for someone who had sold his wine business three years previously but was still receiving an eye-watering tax bill even though his accountant had tried to resolve the issue. One of the other, very regular, roles was providing assistance with internet issues. I am by no means a techie and it really was a case of "in the land of the blind, the one-eyed man is king". What I did know were all the different tests to follow though before contacting the internet provider and which could sometimes resolve the problem. Most people used Orange and I knew how to access the internet, even when not accessible, to check administrator privileges, etc. Another barrier requiring my help would be language issues or the fact that Orange would never return a call to a mobile number that was not French. It proved to be a good little earner as, like me, the clients would hate being out of email circulation for any length of time.

There were many times that I earned money owing to a client's lack of administration. My early years as a secretary provided skills that I continued to use throughout my working life. There was a lovely couple who had a large property and garden and I met them relatively late into my time as a Property Manager. Although they were both adorable, their lives seemed chaotic in relation to paperwork and paying bills. Up until I met them, I had only witnessed one communication from a hussier (*bailiff*) which was linked to a client's utility bill that had gone astray. This contract rolled from reminders of unpaid bills through to bailiff letters with alarming speed. Initially, their property had been managed by a couple who "disappeared" and left one or two people in a mess. The couple had been billing them but in reality only coming and working hard throughout a weekend just prior to the owners' visit. For the rest of the time, they invoiced for work that they were not doing.

At the beginning of the contract, I had no idea that the invoices for the utilities would be so troublesome. Every invoice went to their home address and not their French home. The clients did not have any direct debits arranged for electricity, water or gas and, therefore, relied on sending cheques which would take days to arrive. My only "heads up" would be a letter to the French address advising that the service would be cut off or that the non-payment of the invoice would be passed to a bailiff or, indeed, a letter from a bailiff. The couple spoke some French but were not at a level to understand some of the letters that were received regarding utilities. I suspect letters advising non-payment were not flagged as critical or investigated.

Over time I set up direct debits for all bills and yet even this structure did not negate further issues when insufficient funds were in the bank. The owner had sold his involvement in a wine estate some years previously but the local Treasury had some administrative issues and were still deducting hefty amounts from the client's French bank account causing it to be in credit one minute and in a negative situation the next. He did not do on-line banking so the first flag of an issue would be an unpaid utility direct debit. I was so unfamiliar with clients being threatened by bailiffs that I had a hugely stressful time and I am certain that I took on board the majority of the stress on every occasion.

I recall a letter from a bailiff regarding an overdue gas bill where they recognised it was a holiday home and appreciated it could be unoccupied. They confirmed that this would not deter them and that the owner should note that they had the right to break down the door and take goods to the value of the invoice. I did not doubt that they could do this and I felt sick on behalf of the owner who seemed far too chilled by this declaration! In time, I resolved the on-line banking issues so that the owner could see his current account at all times and "we" gradually got on top of the situation as all bills were managed by monthly direct debits. Year on year, the utility companies had monthly funds going into the account and their relief was probably only second to my own. The only anomaly was the water bill which was managed via the town hall and they did not have a system of monthly direct debits. They still had a bailiff letter for an unpaid water bill at the time I closed the business!

I always felt extremely anxious to see a bailiff's letter or a failed direct debit because of France's banking rules and regulations. I reference the French and money in Chapter One.   I explained these stringent rules to the couple as they seemed so relaxed about the letters and bounced cheques. I suspect the wife was used to her husband's administrative shortcomings and he was not at the house in France and, therefore, not witnessing the issues that I was having to manage on his behalf.

I remember one of the property management tasks was extremely interesting on many levels. The house was owned by Americans who were a warm-hearted couple. They lived in a small cul de sac of old stone properties in a quiet village. Next door to them was a French woman with a penchant for collecting feral cats whose number multiplied with alacrity, together with a whole host of chickens and cockrels. The average chicken coop needs one cockrel, supposedly to keep the girls in order (that remark is making me twitch!), yet this neighbour had at least three of them. Once you introduce competition, the cockrels begin a cacophonous crowing to outdo each other. We're not talking just around five in the morning, we're talking all day long and incessantly. It really could tip you into insanity. The house was a rental property and quite a few people passed comment on the noise if not the smell emitting from the hen house. The owners and I had a meeting with the village mayor who was, understandably, defensive that holiday home owners, who were absent many months of the year, should have reason to complain. He advised that he had approached the neighbour in the past to confirm that she needed to resolve the problem and yet nothing had been done. The immediate neighbours, although individually complaining to the Maire, had all refused to sign a petition to back the clients even though they could not open their windows. They ran in the opposite direction if asked to be involved and it was interesting to see how they would react on an individual basis even though the appeal would have had more strength offered as a community issue.

We had two meetings with the mayor who stressed it was an agricultural village and we were beginning to lose hope of a resolution. The owners paid for me to visit a notaire (*solicitor*) to look into French law. She gave an unhelpful shrug saying that we might be able to get a Health and Safety agent to record noise levels but these were always subjective as to what constituted too noisy. She offered little else that was productive. Fortunately, the visit to the solicitor seemed to shunt the mayor into action and he issued another letter to the neighbour with mention of possible police action. This had the desired effect and she moved all the chickens, cockrels and feral cats to land that she owned in the genuine countryside. Years later, she started up again and my last visit to the house was accompanied by a cockrel chorus. Aie caramba!

Given all the feral cats, it was a surprise that the clients' house was the chosen home of mice during the winter months. The frustrated owner would supply bags of poisonous grains that I would diligently set around the kitchen area and other vulnerable spots. It carried on for years and we took to using traps which were slightly more successful.

Eventually we reached a time when a whole section of the electrics in the house failed. I contacted one of the electrical companies and they despatched a technician. He checked the mains fuse box and a secondary fuse box in the house and everything seemed in order. He then asked if there was a cabling inspection box in the house as the supply to the fuse boxes was broken. This was new terminology to me as I didn't realise they existed. In the end we located it; tucked away in a laundry cupboard. He removed the front plastic protective plate and behind it was a host of chewed wires, mouse poo, and a dead critter or two. All the damaged wires had to be removed and he attached new wiring. Before fixing back the protective plate, he filled the whole box with the insulating spray foam that looked like a giant honeycomb bladder and a certain deterrent to any future rodents. I also remember this house had a light switch problem and when the electrician lifted the cover off, we were greeted by a "fried" and miniscule little gecko that had somehow found a way in …… but not out!

Mice created problems in one or two of the other houses and I was always on the lookout for signs of these unwelcome visitors. Another seasonal "renter" could be wasps! Winters would be mice but long summer months in an unoccupied house could be perfect nesting potential for wasps. When I was doing the house checks, I would often go into each room and look for any irregular activity. I would not open windows or shutters unless airing the house was part of the brief so they could remain shut for several months. One house visit, I remember going into a bedroom and hearing a distinctive buzzing coming from behind the curtains. I went to investigate. To my horror on the outside of the window, in the gap between the window and the wooden shutter, was a huge wasps' nest. It was sufficiently large that I was hyperventilating with earlier memories of a problem when I had a flat in Acton, West London. In that instance I had to call on the fire brigade (in the days when they would still help you for free).

I realised that if I could reach the bracket of the wooden shutter then I could open the wooden panels and the wasps could escape but how to achieve this when the act of opening the window would cause them to fly in! I decided to get a broom handle and open the window the bare minimum and try and push the shutter bar upwards. It took several attempts but I was successful without getting stung. The wasps naturally took exception to having their home exposed to the 39° heat and this aberration created indignant activity where, if they'd formed a chain, I would not have been surprised if they'd have closed the shutter. I knocked away the remains of the nest, feeling a little dejected at their bereavement, and returned the next day to spray the shutter. After this incident, I would regularly open shutters and it was not uncommon to see the small beginnings of a dust coloured mound that heralded the start of a nest.

Another incident, which required professional help, was in a garden where there was a swimming pool with a sliding plastic all-weather hood. The owners would regularly visit the house and benefit from using the pool all year round. The hood's panels were set in steel frames and at one end there was a small transparent doorway to allow access to run a robot or other devices. As I looked around the garden to check everything was in order, my eyes set upon a number of wasps flying around this door. Much to my surprise one or two seemed to be disappearing into the metal which defied logic and curiosity drew me closer. To my amazement the wasps were squeezing into a tiny hole in the metal frame. The whole of the arch was abuzz and they'd found an extremely irregular and odd choice of home. The tubular frame was full of wasps. I waited to ensure my diagnosis was correct and decided that this needed professional intervention as spraying the entrance might not guarantee full removal of the nest. The following week, an agent "guêpes et frelons" (wasps and hornets) came and resolved the problem. It was a first for me but a regular event for him. One of the many tasks that caused my index file of business cards to swell and, throughout the years, people in the village would often stop me to ask if I could recommend a specialist for this or that.

The only other entomological nuisances would be ants, once the warmer weather arrived, or the activity of mites in your wardrobe from February or mosquitoes in the summer. I have never known mites before and I suspect it's a warm country "thing". They could do untold damage chomping on your pashminas or seeking out a nice cashmere sweater. I learned to follow the signs in the supermarket and lay deterrents in wardrobes and drawers in February. The supermarkets can be relied upon to follow the seasons with the necessary products – not all of them fruit and vegetables. An appeal of living in France is the dedicated allegiance to the changing seasons. I am a firm believer that the body works in synch with the planet and that the human engine falters if the rhythm of the two is broken.

Whatever grows in the ground throughout the year is what you will see in the supermarkets. Here in the south, asparagus is abundant in April, cherries in May, followed by nectarines, peaches, melons, etc. These summer fruits give way to the gourds and pumpkins in October who partially relinquish their duties to packaged vegetables to create a Pot-au-Feu or packs of cheese squares to create a raclette in the winter months. Interspersed during these months, you'll find the mini lavender or pine cubes as deterrents to mites, powders and gels against the ants, mosquito repellent and other items required as each season heralds the welcome and the not-so-welcome. On rare occasions, I might be frustrated at the lack of availability of a produce that is available all year around in the U.K supermarkets, where beans arrive from Africa or aubergines from Japan, but these moments are very rare. I am mostly comforted as I walk into a supermarket and realise the first apricots are now available and count my blessings that each season is so defined. It feels right in the most basic of senses.

Returning to the problems caused by insects reminds me of a property in a nearby town that experienced issues from mosquitoes. To the left of the house was a large property owned by a French couple and to the right and under a crumbling archway was a building that had been converted into flats. Access to the cellar of my clients' house was through the archway which was in a perilous state and it also led to a garden to the rear of their house. The garden, which included a partially ruined building, was owned by a young architect who owned the flats but did not live in them. He had no interest in the garden other than sitting on a piece of land that would be worth many thousands of euros at some time in the future when he was ready to sell it. Unfortunately, the flats used the garden to dump their old bicycles, children's unwanted toys and general detritus. However, the worst of the problems were the many tubs and pots that collected rainwater plus the ruined building that had no roof so the stagnant rainwater became a breeding ground for mosquitoes. It got so bad that one of the clients' bedroom windows could no longer be opened and they asked me to try and identify who owned the garden to see if they could buy it. They were eager to create a nice exterior area as they only had a roof terrace and they were upset by the neglect of such a key space in the centre of town.

Eventually, I tracked down the owner and rang him. I explained about the mosquitoes and the rubbish and he acknowledged that he'd asked renters to stop dumping stuff in the garden but that he would tell them again. He did not want to sell the land and, in the event that he ever did, there was already someone who was waiting for it to come onto the market.   I reported back to the owners and waited for the tubs to be emptied but nothing happened. I managed to find his email and sent him a reminder. The water was then emptied a fortnight later but no attempt was made to stop water collecting in the pots in the future or at all on the exposed floor of the ruin. Emails were sent from time to time pleading for the water tubs and pots to be removed or upturned but he never took any ownership of the issue and I even wrote to the Mairie on the clients' behalf to see if they could intervene. After three years of issues, we no longer worried about the standard mosquitoes as the south of France was suddenly home to the Tiger Mosquito that brought diseases such as dengue, Zika, and chikungunya. Many of the Mairies were writing to people advising not to create any areas of stagnant water on their properties. Rather surprisingly, we received no response to my letter from the Maire (*mayor*) so I went to see them. I talked to one of the deputies responsible for Health and Safety matters and he showed zero to no interest in the problem. It was extremely frustrating and was never resolved even at the time of closing my business. I suspect emails are still being sent!

The water and risk of Tiger mosquitoes only paled slightly when the stone archway looked like it would fall on your head at any moment. God knows how the tenants and their children tolerated the danger. I had asked a builder to have a look at it as he was quoting for some work for my clients. He acknowledged the dangerous state, verified that the building above it was independent of the client's house and they were not at risk if the archway did in fact fall. The building directly above the archway was empty (no surprise) but there was a flat on the floor directly above the empty section. The builder explained that he had good contacts within the Mairie which I did not doubt as he often restored listed buildings in the area and his team were real craftsmen. The cellar was accessible via the house, however, log deliveries were one of the many times when I would need to go back and forth under the archway. The builder was true to his word and, to our amazement, over the next 3 months an iron gate was fitted to the only bit of the walls able to support drilling. This stopped the tourists going down the alley to take photographs of this historical part of the town and was undoubtedly the mayor covering himself in the event of an injury claim. The owner left the archway exactly as it was even though there was an occupied property at the very top of it.

The collection of homes that I managed crossed many borders. Clients heralded from the U.K., Ireland, Australia, Italy, Germany, Switzerland, Luxembourg, Sweden, USA, Japan, Belgium, Canada, China, and France (Paris). Towards the latter years, I also included a number of locals who would go away on holiday and want some level of house care, garden watering or pet sitting.

All of these clients had cultural differences. It is easy to generalise but there were some very distinctive traits that must be based on more than just personality. I suppose I could be criticised for over communicating by those who preferred a more relaxed style of property management but I always adopted the principle that, as they paid me, they should know exactly what was happening and how I earned the fee that was invoiced.

The Australians (two sets of clients) were lovely. I was rather surprised at how many Australians had holiday homes in our region. What an incredibly long journey to make. Property in France is not an investment so I could not really see the motivation. I remember sitting in Marseille airport when I struck up a conversation with a man who had just been visiting his holiday home. He had property in New York, Paris, London, Monaco and a tourist village in France. He said the only country where he could make a profit was the United Kingdom. I knew this to be true as I had sold my house in 2003 and just 15 years later its value increased by £175,000. In a similar period, my property in France had increased by the equivalent of £60,000 which did not allow for the considerable investment I had made on many restoration projects such as a new bathroom and roof insulation.

Occasionally, unpleasant clients crept through my radar to become a right headache; albeit a very rare event. A business spanning so many years and with so many clients and cultures would inevitably contain those that were good in which we delighted in the positive times and we commiserated with more challenging incidents. One client sticks out in my mind which no amount of good grace on my part will invoke good memories. He was definitely category "ugly". He was extremely wealthy and had purchased a delightful and sprawling stone house in nearby hilltop village which was a favourite with tourists. He wanted to rent it in the summer months and had been given my name by an estate agent. The property could accommodate up to ten people and could have been a great rental as the house was divine, however, he had little interest in it and would not spend any money whatsoever to maintain the property which is essential when it is a rental; particularly if there is a swimming pool. The irony was that every time he came to the village he stayed in a nearby hotel which was one of the most expensive in the region.

I had a taste of the problems to come when he would not buy enough chairs for the garden or terraces for those wanting to sunbathe. I explained that a large house needed an equivalent number of sun loungers let alone at least one parasol. The email exchange was rude and no amount of explaining could make him realise that it was not a demanding request. Later on fridges broke down, TVs didn't work, the central heating boiler covered the garden chairs and the swimming pool in black soot and the jacuzzi water was dirty for arriving guests. He took no responsibility for any of it and his handyman started to step away from being helpful. On one occasion towards the end of the relationship, I found that I had to ring him (I think it was the incident of soot over the garden during a rental). He called me a range of expletives in English and I remember, in particular, being called a f***ing c***. I was horrified by the language and also that a refined man in his 70's could use such language to a woman. Eventually, I summarised the issues in an email and explained that I could no longer manage the property. I also explained that the use of that language was not acceptable and I wouldn't hesitate to take legal action if he used it again. He put the house back on the market shortly afterwards so maybe he could not rent it or it was some sort of tax loss?

I found Parisian clients could be very demanding (verging on rude) and treated the people of the South rather in the same way as Northern Italians treat the Southerners. The Belgians frustrated the locals as they tended to always import their own artisans and, therefore, provided no economy into their village or the region. The Americans were quite a spectrum of characters and all were totally in love with the mediaeval stone properties. The Swiss were always disciplined and detailed and a perfect descriptive word in French is "carré" (*normally it means square but used this way means clear and decisive*). If you become a Property Manager, you will find the approach you use across the different cultures will vary – or it should!

CHAPTER 7
Managing Break-ins

Unfortunately, during the time of my business there were five clients who suffered break-ins. One of these was with violence which was an alarming insight to how crime had changed in France. It was a far cry from those childhood visits where you could leave your house unlocked and go and see a neighbour. It slowly changed over the years but violence is a phenomenon rarely seen in the South. Of course, holiday homes can make an easy target, in particular the unalarmed houses, but it was very surprising to find one house, recently acquired and still empty, was burgled.

It was a very fortunate event as it turned out. The owners had purchased loads of furniture delivered from a store in Avignon.   I had taken delivery of the boxes at the house which included tables, chairs, kitchen items, and more. As I drove past one day, I realised the security grill in front of the main door was open. On investigation it was clear that the front door had also been forced. Whether they came without decent torches, I don't know. The first room had many signs of builders working inside; boxes of tiles, bags of cement, a variety of tools. Maybe they thought it was a waste of time as they expected to find a furnished home of TVs and other electrical items? It proved a lucky break as all the boxed items remained in place and the only cost was the repair to the door and a new lock.

I am sure that not many break-ins would have supplied boxed items making them very attractive for resale. Years later the clients installed an alarm. The latter can cause its own issues as the Mistral winds, when they blow at 100+ kilometres, can easily set off sensitive alarms – houses, swimming pools, cars, you name it.

Another break-in occurred the day a client left for Geneva. She used to travel there very regularly. Something seemed very strange to me that the very day she left resulted in an attempted break-in. I was the call-out person who the alarm company contacted in the event of an incident. At the time I had a visit from my family and, following a call at one thirty in the morning, my movements above my sister's bedroom caused her to wake up and she decided to come with me. We got to the house and I opened the metal gate for access to the garden and the house. Initially, I could not see any problems. Using the torch on my mobile phone, I scanned the door frame. At that point I realised the whole frame of the door had been prised apart from the wall and I could see into the property. Terrified at the possibility that someone was still in there, I backed off and told my sister to run to the car with me following in hot pursuit. I sat in the locked car and rang the police who arrived pretty quickly and I also rang the owner and the alarm company. Fortunately, the contract provided for a security agent to stay at the house at a daily supplement.

As soon as daylight arrived, I remember calling a carpenter on the Saturday morning who agreed to come out straightaway which was surprising given it was a weekend. Fortunately, I had taken a lot of photographs when he sent a team to refit the door frame and secure the house. Much later the insurance company tried to decline payment as they had not seen the damage before I had authorised the work. I had to send all the photos and remind them that, once the alarm contact on the door was broken, a second visit would have been easy and they would have had to pay out on a huge bill rather than a door repair. I suspect they were affronted but they did cough up the costs of the carpenter's bill which was less than the many thousands they might have had to pay out. I am not too sure what I could have done differently. I suppose I could have had the client pay for a security guard to remain on site 24/7 until an insurance assessor had visited and agreed the repairs. This could have easily taken a week and relied upon the security guard remaining extremely vigilant.

Another break-in was into a garage of a house and items such as a lawnmower and garden tools were taken. A further one was when the clients were actually in their recently built villa and the owner walked downstairs which caused the burglars to flee. It was not before they'd taken a few items which bizarrely included a load of a paperwork which included invoices and guarantees which would later cause all sorts of administrative problems for their newly built home.

I recall a particularly bad occasion when the owner had arrived with his teenage son. It was a house located in the countryside and a good 50 minute drive from my home. He spoke very little French and I managed the house admin, small breakdowns, and the work by the gardener. I got a distressed call, again in the early hours of the morning, advising he had woken up to find someone in a black cagoule leaning over his bed and he had woken to his son shouting. In the bedroom next door, the other disguised intruder was hitting out at the son who was trying to prevent his rucksack from being taken. Both intruders made off into the night which was just as well as the house owner was ex-military and of firm build. They tried to take his hire car but it needed a credit card type key to start it and they had no idea what to do.

I shot over to the house having called the police on the owner's behalf. I acted as interpreter to explain the details of the attack to the three gendarmes. Two were dressed in the usual blue gendarme uniform and one man was suited and booted. He explained that he was a crime specialist. He felt certain the incident was linked to a gang operating out of Nimes and maybe 20 members strong. The members would go to the large outdoor markets and listen out for English and other foreign languages being spoken. They then followed the tourists' cars back to their homes. Fortunately, the losses were not too great for the owner. They had taken his wallet and so all credit cards had to be cancelled and the cash had gone.

They also took a camera. The situation could have been a lot worse. As the adrenalin stopped pumping on the drive back home, I did briefly consider that maybe I should apply to the French police to act as an interpreter. In the end, I did not do anything about it.

I had one other incident which proved to me that my life was more important than putting myself in the line of fire and before I gave up being an alarm contact - other than in daylight hours. A Swiss chap had installed his own video alarm system. He rang around two in the morning to advise the alarm had triggered on his mobile but he could not see anyone as obviously it was dark in the house and outside. I went down to investigate. I was in front of the villa and rang the police. That was when I learned that they would not come out to help you unless you saw evidence of a break-in such as forced windows, doors, shutters. I found myself talking to a police control centre in Paris, several hundred miles away. They told me to investigate around the outside of the property. I confirmed that I was on my own, it was pitch dark and, being a woman, I was hardly able pack a good punch. I insisted he stay on the phone line and, if he heard me scream, then he was to take appropriate action. He had the address. I can remember him saying "Allons y, Madame" (the equivalent of "*off you go*"). Jeez, thanks mate!

As it turned out, there were no signs of anything sinister. The owner decided a spider had walked across the sensor. This incident, followed by the previously mentioned scenarios, was sufficient for me to stop house alarm checks at night. I highly recommend that you either only act as the point of contact for the alarm companies who send out their own agents when an alarm triggers or you only agree to be involved during the hours of daylight.

During the years that I had the business, it was inevitable that there would be times when the bad news might not simply relate to technical breakdowns or minor incidents. It was important to know how to communicate bad news to the owners who might live within Europe but could equally be as far away as Japan, Australia or the United States. I have attached an Appendix that provides my own style of communicating what could potentially be alarming news for the recipient.

Apart from the break-ins, I worked on one major flood, two fires, assisted with the sale of five homes, had seven deaths of home owners/partners, six property purchases and saw five new additions to the families.

Chapter 8
Property Fires

Occasionally, I would benefit from increased income through the saddest of situations that I would not wish upon anyone. I remember being awoken by a phone call from a man who was the gardener/handyman of a client's chateau. I was at least an hour's drive away and he lived in the same village as the property. He had gone to open up the windows of the chateau in order to air the building and to do some gardening in the sprawling park. The call informed me that there had been a fire and that a number of rooms were impacted by black smoke. The poor visibility made it difficult to determine the full extent of the damage and what had happened. The firemen had been called and were on their way. I rearranged my planned day and sped up to the property.

It was clear that a battery charger, used by an electrician, had overheated and created a fire up a wall in a corridor. Although, luckily, the flames did not catch and move out of the corridor, the ensuing black smoke moved from the passageway into a bedroom, a bathroom, the chateau's main reception room, the music room and two other corridors. Even with all the windows open, the smell was atrocious and the walls, furniture, and floors were black with smoke damage. This was particularly upsetting given the wallpaper in the main reception room was 18th century. All those years of sitting there in splendour to be ruined by 21st century improvements to restore the property to its former glory.

I notified the owner and set about contacting the insurance company who sent an assessor even though the rooms had to sit for several days untouched to preserve the "evidence". Fortunately, they had worked with many prestigious buildings in France and had a talented network of specialist contacts. These specialists confirmed that they thought the wallpaper would be salvageable which was heartwarming.

The property had a network of external and internal cameras so I checked the footage to see if there was anything captured on disc. In the early years, the system was always problematical but it did capture the smoke moving through the rooms. There was no sprinkler system installed as the chateau had many fine paintings and objet d'art so this could have caused considerable damage. After the events of the fire, the alarm system was upgraded to include smoke sensors.

The electrician repeatedly said that the charger was not switched on. I found that hard to believe given it would be a logical sequence of events to work all day and then put items on charge. He had become a good friend to the owner and a hard worker so I was reassured that he was in touch with his insurer as he was definitely not denying responsibility.

For my part, I liaised with the insurer's recommended companies who would clean all the floors, walls, furniture, chandeliers, sconces, rugs, electrical equipment, etc. and a timeline was agreed. The electrician's wife attended a number of meetings with the insurers to support her husband and she would most definitely have fought his corner if required. The insurers, realising a huge bill would be coming their way, insisted that I obtain an Attestation from the fire brigade who attended the chateau. It was, of course, another first for me as I drove to the fire station to have a meeting with the Chef de Brigade. I quizzed him if an unplugged battery charger could burst into flames. In typical French fashion he mused on it being possible in some cases although it was rare. He could not categorically say one way or the other. The report noted the seat of the fire and the condition of the charger and noted it was unplugged but that this was still the perceived cause. The insurers were accepting of the document and liaised with the electrician's insurer to recoup their costs. I don't want to imagine what the poor guy's next annual business insurance fee would come to.

Over time the sorrowful building saw the care of the workers spin their magic and, bit by bit, each room returned to its original splendour. The owner came over mid clean-up and was stoic in accepting the tragedy and equally relieved that the wall paper in the reception room was eventually returned to its original splendid state. Understandably, he saw this as the biggest potential loss, one which would have been intolerable. The electrician remained working at the chateau for which, I imagine, he was extremely grateful. His distress did not reduce until he saw the property return by degrees to the state before the fire. Although British, the owner had lived in the USA for many years so that his approach to artisans was definitely to boot them out if they messed up. I think it might have been borne from the amount of Mexican labourers readily available in his region. Fortunately, given the excellence of the electrician's work and his great mind for problem solving new home comforts in centuries old castles, he stayed employed!

There was one other occasion when a client property had a fire, however, this was luckily restricted to the garden where a bamboo hedge caught fire owing to the old halogen garden lights heating up all the dead leaves. As you will see in the next chapter, there was also a time when I had to manage a property flood so I have added my methodology of handling property disasters in the Appendix.

Chapter 9
Dealing with Floods

Some years after the fire, I was to contact the very same specialists who had worked on the chateau clean-up for yet a further catastrophe. A delightful couple of Australian women, who were close friends in Melbourne, had fallen in love with a beautiful town house in a beautiful mediaeval town. They took it in turns to come over and would often stay a month or more. One of the owners came over in January 2012. She left at the end of the month and I was next due to go to the house at the end of February. The month of February had started badly with one of the worst cold snaps that the South had seen and certainly the coldest that I have experienced to date. We suffered minus 4 during the day and minus 12 at night. It went on for days. Temperatures like this had not been seen since 1956 when fields of olive groves were decimated together with the vines. Ironically many of the exported vines sent to the U.S.A in earlier times were reintroduced back to the South of France in attempts to restart vine growing following the '56 disaster.

My first knowledge of the problem came via the estate agent who had sold the house to them. A cascade of water had been pouring out of the brickwork at the top of the house and falling in a theatrical yet beautiful waterfall of ice down onto a neighbour's terrace. The neighbour had gone to the local Mairie on Friday afternoon to explain it was a holiday home and no one was there. The Mairie said that they had no responsibility for activity inside properties and advised that they would take no action. All weekend the water continued to run. The neighbour, feeling certain that this was a grave situation, must have asked around and eventually located the name of the estate agent who had sold the house.

On a fateful Tuesday morning, I got a phone call from the agent. She explained that water was still pouring through the brickwork on the upper side of the house which would have been the kitchen (owing to spectacular views, this was an upside-down house where the kitchen was on the top floor). I went to the house and nervously opened the door. Three things struck me immediately. Everything was dark and no lights worked (owing to negativity of water and electrics), the noise of running water, and the smell! I think I was hoping for a split pipe in the kitchen but I hadn't thought through the house configuration. I was greeted with a disaster. Owing to the water running for so long, the kitchen was flooded and had soaked through the floor, this had brought down a section of the ceiling in the sitting room below and the tiled floor was an ice rink and it was extremely difficult to stay upright. Going down to the next floor, water was running through the beamed ceiling over the entire bedroom and had also turned the floor into a skating rink.

Down again to the ground level and water was running through the ceiling and covering furnishings and fittings. In my frozen stupor, I was trying to comprehend the origin of the water until I realised that the water had not been turned off. The owner had omitted to disconnect the water when she left and my next visit was scheduled after the flood had occurred. Once I had disconnected the water I tried to clear the fog of panic to digest what needed to be done. I contacted a friend to come and help me as I needed to mop up vast amounts of water even though the floors had turned to ice. The central heating boiler, which had been problematic since ownership, could not be lit even though it was fed by mains gas.

I knew of the insurance company so I put a call out to them which, owing to the increased workload, was not an immediate visit and I returned home to compose an email to the owners. I remember thinking long and hard about how to phrase it as they would be opening it at the start of their day. I began with all the actions that I had taken, very much in the vogue of a Project Manager, and then explained the sequence of events leading up to my discovery.

The insurance assessor eventually arrived together with a senior representative of the boiler maintenance company. After all, the boiler was set to manage a frost setting and should have switched on. There were endless discussions on the maintenance service which had been done six weeks previously and the boiler's overall condition given it was not particularly old. The assessor left firmly telling me that, as Property Manager, I could well be held accountable. The boiler maintenance representative was categorically denying responsibility. I explained that I was not expected to visit the house until the end of the month and that the owner had, unfortunately, not switched off the water. He was having none of it. After they had left, these parting comments, together with the condition of the house, reduced me to tears and I sat on a dry chair and balled my eyes out for a good fifteen minutes.

On the news that the insurance company might want to go after me, I contacted the owner. Thanks to her considerate and glowing email taking full responsibility, the insurance assessor could not attribute any blame to me.

I had set up meetings with IDEM; the company who done such sterling work at the chateau. I remember they used another company who came and took all the TVs and electrical items as they needed drying out, testing etc. Another agent came and took all the rugs and small carpets.

The process to return the house back to normal took months. The plaster of the new ceiling could not be done immediately and we then had to wait for it to dry. The painter had also advised that the stone walls needed at least 3 months to dry out before he could clean the water traces that had caused the creamy coloured stone to turn brown. In July and August it would have been a matter of weeks to dry the house but this was a problem in February and with a boiler that did not work. I took gilded mirrors that had crumbled with water damage to specialist antique repairers and I went to dry cleaners with bag loads of quilts and duvets needing to be dry cleaned. Eventually, the insurers paid the bills but they deducted 30% from the total costs as the water had not been disconnected and they pushed back against many invoices until I could get further clarification from the artisans on the specifics of their work. I really expected them to pay a lot less and it highlighted that many holiday home owners really do not know the small print of their contracts. I checked my own as a permanent owner and tried to anticipate future problems for clients whilst appreciating that no two insurance companies, or their rules, are the same.

Chapter 10
Artisans

I wouldn't want you to think that I rolled from one disaster to another. This was most certainly not the case and the average month would be taken up with house checks and occasionally arranging for ad hoc repairs to be done, watering courtyards or gardens, programming automatic watering systems, topping up swimming pool water levels, etc. Usually after owner visits, there would be increased activity particularly if they had decided to do restoration work.

Sometimes my house checks could provide humorous memories such as when I had to scoop out a tiny, live pipistrelle bat that had landed in a swimming pool and been washed into the skimmer basket. The sensation of this tiny Dracula on my bare skin was gag inducing but I achieved the desired result and it flew off to recover from its ordeal.   The key fob for that house was renamed as "International Bat Rescue". I was holding about 30+ keys and I never had the owners' names on them in case they were mislaid. It was part of a great game I played to name each one with something that would make them instantly recognisable to me but not to anyone else. Among the names were aliases such as "Cartoons", "Gruyere", "Ducati" and "Marshmallow".

One of the competencies that can make or break a Property Manager is finding good artisans; workmen who can react quickly and sometimes at weekends.

A property manager needs to find great contacts in a minimum of six skills. It helps to develop a relationship where they know you will give them the time to start and complete jobs that are not urgent and educate them as to what "urgent" means in relation to your understanding and the clients' homes. The five artisan roles are: builder, plumber, electrician, carpenter, locksmith and pest control.

When I first started the role, I would use a plumber/electrician who lived in my village. Commonly, plumbing and electrical breakdowns seldom provide early warnings of their imminent failure. When I called the artisan, he would normally advise that he would come to the house the next day at nine o'clock which would be music to my ears, however, this would soon dissipate as the minutes passed by the next day. After half an hour, I would ring and he'd say "oh, I can't do it today, I'll come tomorrow". This meant that a client had paid for my time and the problem was not fixed and they'd be paying again tomorrow. I explained to him numerous times that I had to charge for my time, like he did, and that him changing the dates and not telling me meant my client was paying for nothing. This did not even dent his ability to continue in the same vein until I realised he was a liability and adding unnecessary charges to oversee breakdowns.

Through the small village network, I heard of a young plumber who had recently moved into the area. I decided to try him out. Oh the joy of someone who actually turned up when expected, worked efficiently and through to completion of the task (no missing days). It is quite a rare characteristic in France as one bit sometimes is missing. I explained that I managed many holiday homes, which for me would have been a green light to a lot of potential work, yet to him was a shrug following by "eh, oui?" Fortunately, he and I worked together for many years. His only foible was to constantly talk to himself whilst he worked. After the sixth time of walking into a room saying "désolée, je n'ai pas entendu" (*sorry, I didn't catch that*?), I realised that this was a trait to be ignored – that and the out of tune whistling. Over time, I demonstrated to him that I would give him time for the jobs that were not urgent, and when Gill said "this is really urgent", he would respond accordingly and often come to a house immediately. This is the nub of finding and keeping good artisans. Never "cry wolf" like so many home owners. The French artisans do not ask "how high" when you say "jump". They are more likely to say "va chier" ("piss off" or worse!)

The previous plumber was also an electrician so it was a loss, in more ways than one, when he messed around with dates and times to fix problems. I needed to replicate the reliability of "my" new plumber with an equally dedicated electrician. This happened by chance when I found a business card in one of the client's letterboxes in a nearby village. Sometimes, I would trial an artisan for one problem and, if good, they stayed in my "contacts" list.

This electrician was of a similar age to the plumber, equally efficient, and had a pleasing personality, and he quickly became a close working colleague. Both of them worked with me in the knowledge that I would not abuse the urgency of a job and a mutual respect was more than evident. I would need both of them at weekends if there were problems with rental houses as inevitably the changeover day would be Saturdays in July and August. I would dread hearing a renter say on the morning of checkout that they'd had a problem with the drains since their arrival - even though a call during the week could have resolved it rapidly and effectively. This meant, with people arriving late afternoon, I had to draw on artisans who normally would not answer a mobile on a weekend so the relationship with these two young guys became even more crucial. I think they were representative of a changing trend. The older artisans would always have a steady stream of work as they'd built up a clientele over the years that were faithful to them. When one job finished, there was always another one in the pipeline. The young "pups" were after that work and applied a level of customer service that was rather alien to their aged compatriots. The plumber and electrician were a great find and I know that they often recommended each other when working on people's homes that did not belong to my clients.

One of the jobs which, fortunately, "my" young plumber avoided was following a huge storm in our village. The torrential rainfall that can occur at the break of summer and usually three or four times a year are known as «épisodes cévenols». These incredible storms with their deluge of rainfall ensured that it was not uncommon to see bad flooding. The ground was baked hard from the summer heat and the rain bounced off the impenetrable ground which was unable to absorb it at the speed it was falling. The average amounts of water could vary between 200 and 400 mm and the drains could not adequately clear it in time. This was never helped if those drains had remained untouched for months resulting in the roots of trees and shrubs impacting the water clearance. Never grow oleander bushes near septic tanks, swimming pools or mains water drainage. They are the most beautiful of colourful shrubs throughout the south of France and yet they will weave their roots under the plastic collars joining two pipes and create untold damage. I got a lot of work from oleander bushes!

After one of these storms, I would follow up with house checks. There could be anything from roof leaks, window leaks, water under front door frames – et al. It was a blisteringly hot day and I was in my shorts, Property Management polo shirt, and flip-flops ; standard garb for the summer months. I opened the door and stepped into the front room. I was instantly attacked by the smell and also by the fact that my feet were soaking wet. Water was lying through the sitting room, dining room, kitchen, shower room, and corridors. On closer inspection I was wading through effluent water. Yuck ! Owing to the immediate detritus around the trap in the shower room floor, it was obvious that this was where the rainwater had created a problem and caused sewer pipes to back up into the house. Fortunately, there was an old water bill in amongst the post as ringing a utility company without a client reference number was tantamount to asking if you could deliver your Granny to live with them indefinitely.

SAUR is the mains water supplier throughout most of France and fortunately the invoice had their breakdown number. They explained they would respond during the day but that the workload was exceptionally high owing to the storm. I gave them my mobile number to avoid billing any further hours and returned home to contact the client. Many hours later, I got the call to appear at the house. The technicians looked grim faced as they trod through the reeking water and acknowledged "ce n'est pas normal" (*that's not normal*). To give them their due, they enthusiastically disappeared into the street and heavy duty pumping and whooshing ensued until the water level disappeared back to normal and the floors of the house just had residual nasty stuff on them. They advised that they would arrange for all the floors to be professionally cleaned with anti-bacterial product and a specialist would contact me which he duly did.

Apart from the storms, another area that created regular work for me was due to the Mistral wind which played havoc with TV satellite dishes. Most of the holiday homes had Freeview boxes to watch TV in their native language. It was simply a case of positioning the head of the satellite to capture your choice of European language. I learned that just a millimeter out would be sufficient to cause a snowstorm effect on the TV screen or lose the channel completely. The dish, combined with a wind which could reach 120 kilometers, was sufficient to move these ridiculously sensitive saucers on a regular basis. I had my own issues at my house as it was stuck up on the roof and exposed to a regular battering. After the fifth intervention of 80 euros, I decided that I had had enough and relocated it to the side of the house where it aggrieved my aesthetic eye. The addition of changing from a metal dish to a fibreglass dish plus a couple of tension wires was sufficient to do away with any further problems. It just looked so ugly on the side of my stone house and was a constant declaration that old and new cannot always sit well together.

Finding a TV antennist would be another challenge. Not all of them worked with foreign houses and I would find myself explaining the role of the Freeview box and the typical satellite provider as they never knew if the dish operated on Hotbird, Astra or one of the myriad of other possible satellites. If they didn't get it, they were scrapped off my contact list. Another negative attribute could be their overall size and their feet! Most of the dishes were up on roofs and get a 95kg bloke in size 13 boots up there and you were set for a leaky roof the next time that it rained. I managed quite a few new installations and needed to have a certain level of understanding of the electrical cabling of the house if new TV sockets were required. For a house with no existing TV installation, it could be a costly business.

Other reliable and trustworthy support was required in the expertise of carpenters and locksmiths. I established an excellent locksmith contact via a suggestion from a gendarme investigating a break-in. The company that I used on a regular basis were an hour's drive away so they were not immediately close to my client base. Their relationship with the gendarmeries meant that I felt reassured that they were fully trustworthy and when they gave you the new keys to door locks, they didn't have a spare in their back pocket to give to an unscrupulous oik some months later. Carpenters were also running along a parallel track when these events occurred and I tended to use just one or two who also reacted to tight deadlines.

Over the years, I got to understand the typical rate payable for standard breakdowns but I never got used to the high cost of locksmiths in France. It is an area that continues to surprise me but what price can you put on security? I had a number of occasions when keys broke in locks which was always challenging and guaranteed to create a frenzy – particularly if a cat was behind the door waiting to be fed. I remember when a lock broke in the holiday home of a German couple. The key to an old style mortice lock just went around and around and would not engage. The lock was butrussed up against the exterior door frame so there was no leverage to force the door. I rang the owners to advise that I would need to call out my preferred locksmith and got their consent. Although I watched him like a hawk, I still do not know how he opened the door. He found some magical way to get the slipped mechnism inside the lock housing to engage and "hey presto" we were in. After that, he swapped out the old lock for a new one and showed me how the structure had broken and fallen to the base of the lock. I forwarded a new key onto the owners who eventually also received an eye watering invoice.

I became adept in certain areas of breakdowns. There could often be problems with the hard water in our region. This would cause calcium build up that would affect toilets, water heaters, taps and kettles. It would not be unusual for calcium to build up in toilet cisterns causing the granules to get into the ballcock mechanism and for water to continue running through the toilet. I would know how to take off the cistern lid, which was not always evident, and rub down the plastic components to clear the calcium. In nine out of ten cases, the problem was resolved. The tenth occasion usually meant a new mechanism. I would remind people to switch off the water, flush the cisterns so they could not refill, and then the possibility of calcium build-up would be removed but there was always a lot to do when leaving a house so it became an area that I added to my house checks on their departure.

Another area was electrical faults. Fuseboxes would trip out and renters would ring complaining they had no electrics. I would go to the property and complete a basic routine of dropping all fuses on the box. I would then reconnect each fuse slowly and one by one. Eventually, the rogue fuse that was tripping everything in the house would be identified. Usually, this was in an area that meant I had no need to call out an emergency electrician at some ungodly cost. I would get 99% of the house functioning again and advise that I would have an electrician come and sort the problem as rapidly as possible. Holding a key meant that none of the renters nor their holidays were ever impacted.

In thinking about artisans and weekends, I recall a charming electrician who was listed in France's Pages Jaunes (*Yellow Pages*). I had been helping at a meeting for the sale of a client's house and the new owners had asked if I could work for them. They completed the sale on a Friday afternoon and we were in the midst of an épisode cévenol with high storms and lashings of rain. I got a desperate call the following morning to announce they had no electrics in the house. I started to ring around as it was a house that was a long way from my home and I tended to use the contacts provided by the home owner. Naturally no one was happy to pick up a call on a Saturday morning except for one man who would have no idea how profitable his willingness to answer his phone might be.

He came to the house and found no fault with the installation. I had mentioned to him that I had a niggling concern that the house was affected if the water table got too high. He confirmed that this could be the case and the ground would need to dry for the supply to function again. Whilst checking the box, it became clear that many of the fuses were holding five or six cables and others just had one cable which caused the fuses to be overloaded. We agreed for him to rewire as necessary. Fortunately, in the afternoon, the supply returned and it proved to be the case that, if there were exceptionally heavy storms, the electrics would not function for a few hours. Although he had listed himself in the "electrician" category, he was in fact a French builder; a very good builder. Once the clients and I could see the quality of his work and his pricing, he was engaged in the future and that one phone call on a Saturday resulted in him getting a huge amount of work that ran into many thousands over the years:

Insulate and fit a new roof
Replace rotten timbers in the attic
Repoint the façade of the house
Paint five of the rooms
Fit a new bathroom
Repair air-conditioning units
Build and equip a summer kitchen near the swimming pool
Rebuild a pergola
Install a damp course in the guesthouse
Lay a new car park
Repaint the interior of swimming pool and retile mosiac frieze
Rewire several garden lights
Tree maintenance

I think this incredible workload perfectly demonstrates the merits of always being available and not letting your mobile phone go to message service at weekends. Out of the 20+ calls that I made on that fated Saturday morning, only five electricians bothered to ring me back. Thank heavens he picked up his phone. I don't doubt he also reflected on the value of responding being many €€€€ !

One of the skills that I found difficulty locating was a general handyman. There are a few across France but nothing like as many as in Britain. Many of the jobs didn't need a fully trained artisan yet finding someone to repair a panel in a fence or paint around a replaced pane of glass in a window could be frustrating. There were many of those day-to-day niggles that didn't need someone who might charge 30+ euros an hour. In the beginning, if I was capable, I took on the tasks myself, however, starting something that was small would usually turn into something that was bigger and I would not recommend it. I found one or two handymen but they always wanted cash so that meant no guarantees against a future problem let alone the matter of the Trésor and false accounting. Although the wheels on the bus in France need the occasional bit of cash, it was important for owners to know that they could also be fined if it was proven that they had paid an artisan in cash with no invoice for a job.

I located a good handyman but then he moved out of the region and on it went and I was never wholly successful in this area. An Englishman and his wife have just arrived in my village and he is very adept at D.I.Y. and I've encouraged him to start up a small business in this field. France is crying out for handymen and the new business model makes it all so much easier to achieve. I also know a Property Manager/handyman who was schooled in France and so has an excellent command of written and spoken French. He has taken a number of French plumbing and electrical exams and is now fully qualified. The world is his oyster!

Chapter 11
Rentals

Sometimes, in the interests of helping potential clients, I could lose out financially. I got wiser as time went by. One of these examples was the service of advising owners about renting out their home. As mentioned, a French person in my village happily sucked all the information from me and then chose to manage his own rentals the next year. After that experience, I charged a nominal fee to offer this advice and I probably had a half dozen or so occasions when I didn't manage the full rental process but just acted as a consultant before the French family managed their own process.

I would get enquiries either through word of mouth or via estate agents. Many holiday home owners would return to the estate agent to see if they managed seasonal rentals or if they could recommend someone. The French property owners would go to an estate agent as their first port of call to find someone. I soon found that my client base over the years often included six or seven rental houses. This was a business which caused me to be stuck every April to the end of September in France and working every weekend. A chore that I was happy to relinquish many years later.

The rentals aspect of the business would become a regular, and profitable income. I would build adverts on rental web sites, handle the enquiries and bookings, issue contracts, do the check-in and check-outs of renters, and manage the inevitable electrical and plumbing breakdowns. In the beginning I used to clean during the Saturday changeovers for one or two properties. This was never much fun on back-to-back rentals and, in time, with the owners, we interviewed local people to take over this role and to also do the laundry.

Finding local help was always problematical. For the most part it was to find cleaners who could also do the laundry and later it was to find help to do the meet and greet and check-outs. Most of those interested wanted cash and would not accept cheques. They did not want to sign a contract and, therefore, the stress of zero accountability was a source of much concern. I remember at least one young girl informing me on a July Friday night that she was going to the beach with her family the next day so could not clean the rental house. She knew exactly the problem that she was causing for me but there was little I could do about it other than replace her at the earliest opportunity.

As mentioned, I could see strong cultural differences in the international range of holiday home clients. I saw the same country specific traits in the renters. Between 2003 and 2018, I usually had at least 6 rental properties; some houses were sold or stopped renting but other houses backfilled the gaps and replaced the clients. On the whole, the Brits were the most sought after as they were always so respectful of people's houses which they left clean, albeit "used", on check-out. The Dutch tended to just walk out –

house dirty, breakfast items spilling out of the sink, traces of breakfast over the tables. The French adopted the "I've paid for it therefore this house is mine" approach. The Americans were always appreciative and totally in love with the ancient stone houses and yet every American I met remained terrified of using gas canisters as most villages didn't have mains gas. Considering Summer Camps are such a big thing in the USA, I am not sure why there was such fear. The Swiss would clean the house even though this was included in the rental. For the rest, it was a mixed bag.

Fortunately, no one ever had a bad rental and the houses had some great tourist reviews which certainly brought increased business. There was one exception, however, with a house that I took on late into the business years. It was like a gaudy car boot sale with yellow and pink plastic flowers in the bathroom, a myriad of knick-knacks collecting grease and dust in the kitchen and the sitting room; generally a disaster. I was shedding labour intensive work at the time and maybe I needed to backfill my income? It was a stupid decision to take on this house. I managed it for one year and no-one enjoyed their stay and the French owner would never accept any criticism or make any overture to address complaints. Now that everyone has access to TripAdvisor and other feedback sites, you just can't afford to be defensive and ignore rental comments. A bad review of a newly launched rental property is the kiss of death and ignored at your peril. Of course, some reviews are blindingly unfair and a shock when they are sent after a face to face "it's been marvellous, thank you so much" scenario. People are the same worldwide, the majority wait until they've left to either reaffirm a wonderful stay or give it you, both barrels, hiding behind the distance between you.

One of the services I offered was to assess houses for rental and inform owners of what would be required. In the event that I received an enquiry, or that a person was ready to proceed, I would forward a copy of the email noted in the "Appendix" at the end of the book.

I drew up a comprehensive list of the costs that would be involved to rent a property. These would need to be offset against any rental income which proved illuminating to many who just saw the potential revenue of an empty house when they were not using it. This meant that renting some of the smaller village houses proved unviable. The owners would have been doing it for nothing or recuperating maybe a few hundred euros a year whilst putting the house under the pressures of people using it. During rentals, any electrical or plumbing issues had to be resolved quickly and efficiently and all would detract from the rental profit. Pools remained a total bugbear as they had to be pristine and so many were in unsuitable gardens with oleander leaves and flowers falling in the water every few seconds; one was sited right under a hedge of leylandii so was perpetually full of detritus. I quickly developed pool maintenance skills such as completing a backwash or identifying electrolyser problems until the day that I got sick of sweeping the floor of huge pools in 38 degree full sun. One of the areas that, as time went by, I kissed goodbye to as I sought to minimise the outdoor activities in the hottest months of July and August.

Some rental owners chose to say that electricity would be charged based on usage. This was a smart move if the house had air conditioning. It meant that the renters would use the air conditioning intelligently and would certainly not leave the machines running all day whilst they were at the beach or when they were outside drinking an evening apéro. One or two others charged for the supply of bedding and towels. I was not a fan of setting a rental fee, which would appear on the web site search, and then adding a load of supplementary charges in the description field. It put people off; particularly if they had a set budget and had searched within the parameters of their budget.

When I had these rental meetings, usually the clients would want to go ahead relatively quickly as they could often be visiting their house for just a few days and be about to return to their homeland. It was imperative that I went prepared and, apart from taking photographs thus having my camera to hand, I also had a checklist to ensure I captured as many facts as possible. You can find it as an appendix at the end of the book.

Some clients with a house capacity of one or two bedrooms were keen to suggest settees that could be converted into sofa beds and try to advertise the house to appeal to larger numbers. Having seen the impact of renting, I would normally try to persuade them against this decision. Any house has a maximum level of occupancy before it starts "working" too hard. I appreciate that can sound odd but it is definitely true that the amount of wear and tear on a property, the furnishings and the equipment will suffer if it is regularly abused by too many drawing on the facilities. The number of bedrooms is usually the best indicator. Many renters of larger properties were attracted when there were a number of interior or exterior nooks and crannies to provide space and moments of quiet isolation rather than being "on top" of each other all the time.

With so many rental web sites available, I soon began to determine the ones that reached the widest audience. Some small sites were useless and would offer great incentives to try and increase the number of properties in their portfolio. I received all sorts of emails offering a year's subscription for the cost of 6 months or very attractive discounts on multiple properties. Unfortunately, one look at their web site and how many houses they had in the region told me all that I needed to know. There still remains only a handful of top players. It's tough being a small holiday rental site and usually the successful ones are where someone in a different European country, e.g. Germany, targets France and makes that their only market and all the homes are described in German making them instantly attractive to their audience and finding a niche market alongside the "big players".

At the beginning the holiday rental web sites were all offered on an annual subscription, however, over the years and possibly due to the wide choice available, sites began to offer a pay-per-reservation model. This meant that there was no fee to add a property onto their site, however, they would deduct a % per booking and a further % if you allowed benefits to renters such as paying for a booking by credit card. It was a variable amount for each reservation as it was based on the season (summer being more attractive than winter), the number of people versus house capacity, the region and the rental price. Where possible, if an annual subscription existed, then I would always encourage this version. You had a set fee that did not change through the year and could be recouped within the first reservation. For the most part I used "HomeAway" and "Airbnb". The former currently reaches 21 countries but it has been bought by Expedia and I have heard one or two negative remarks yet their coverage continues to be one of the best.

There are also a raft of regional companies that rent properties in specific areas and can be competitive. I often worked with clients who had their house advertised via the web sites that I chose and also used one or two additional companies. This could be frustrating when the owners were not good communicators and I'd take a booking only to find out the house was already rented via one of the competitor companies. It was not unknown for me to send an email at the end of each month to verify the status of bookings to ensure that I was as up to date as possible. I enjoyed describing the appeal of the various rental houses and ensuring the photos were as attractive as possible. You only have to go onto one of the many rental sites to see how dire some of the photography can be or how limiting or unimaginative the property description.

One of the by-products of advertising a house on a recognised holiday home web site can be the incentive for scammers. The modern day plague. All web sites stress the importance of only communicating via their site but it was amazing how creative some of the miscreants could be. As an example, I would have an automatic link to my mobile 'phone if anyone enquired about a property. It was an early flag for me to check availability and respond. This was critical as each web site had all sorts of metrics measuring how fast my response to an enquiry would be, how often I declined a booking, etc. Occasionally, I would get a text to my mobile with a request for dates but then nothing would appear in the "in-box" on the web site. I would contact them with caution and, nine times out of ten, they wanted to pay direct but wanted the bank details first and other data which I could only imagine would be sold somewhere on the open market.

I always issued a rental contract to protect the owners and also the renters. It allowed me to spell out the specific Terms and Conditions and to ensure there was no responsibility for any damage or accidents to individuals with particular attention to swimming pools. Contact with renters could be tricky when web sites did not allow visibility to phone numbers or email addresses. I also appreciated this level of security to avoid enquiries from the scammers. I became quite inventive, together with the rental contact, in being able to achieve an email address and obtain a signed contract.

Contracts would be available in English or in French. With the English contracts, I always added a request for the words "lu et approuvé" to be added (which means the contract *has been read and approved*). This is French law and, given the properties were based in France, I felt that this would ensure any litigation was in the owners' favour. Fortunately, this never ever happened but I felt reassured to see the words always added to the signed English contracts.

One of the other areas that could reduce check-in time or multiple phone calls, was the creation of an A-Z house file per rental property. This covered everything from the internet password to what to do with the dustbins. A house "bible" was invaluable and I produced them in French and English. I never needed other languages as most people had a smattering of English to be able to cope. My schoolgirl German would never have cut the mustard or as they say "gewachsen sein"!

I had a few houses that could sleep six people or more. The larger groups would often want to split up and do different sightseeing trips and, therefore, returned to the property at different times. If a house can sleep more than six then it is not unreasonable to provide two sets of rental keys and a second electric gate fob. These are the differences that make the stay more comfortable and ensure the house is remembered and recommended. I would make a point of explaining two sets of keys rather than one at the check-in so that people remembered these extra facilities. I hoped it would lead to a flattering house review at the end of their stay as good reviews were pivotal to future business.

Rentals in High Season, being July and August for most owners, would always demand a higher price. This eight week period is the peak time to expect a house to be booked as long as the rental fee is sensibly priced. In order that there were no lost weeks or gaps where the house was unoccupied, it was not uncommon for rentals to run from Saturday to Saturday. This meant that someone looking to book Tuesday to Tuesday would not result in the house being empty until the next weekend when most people travelled to rental accommodation. Most renters accommodated this practice and it was the only certain way to ensure owners maximised on rentals during these two critical months.

As revealed, most rentals went without hiccup and with great feedback. It was clearly a reflection of the house and exterior space but also because I was acting as Property Manager and, therefore, I knew the houses and their foibles inside out. I also managed the rentals in the same detailed manner and was the renters' point of contact. The slightest problem and I would be, at the least, on the end of a mobile phone or, at best, at the house within an hour or two. I often had to ring car hire companies or ticket offices owing to language problems. One or two had thefts from hire cars that needed me to liaise with police for the corresponding claim forms for their insurers. Other than swimming pool cleanliness issues, the only other guaranteed area that would create concern would be the loss of an internet connection.

I would go as far as saying that it is now almost impossible to rent a house without an internet connection. It is expected by everyone. Sometimes in the smaller villages where the user numbers are higher than the network can support, even out of High Season, the hordes of visitors invading the rental homes can combine to make an unstable village internet connection. To then add just one family who have three mobile phones, three tablets and a laptop just creates a recipe for problems. Children were the biggest complainers in these instances and it was sad to hear their complaints and see their anxious faces when the area had such a wealth of treasures and beaches to explore.

A role that I was extremely happy to stop after the many years of rentals was the check-ins. I would ensure that I had the arrival time guaranteed (give or take 15 minutes), both mobile phone numbers had been communicated and I always advised that I had several check-ins to do on a Saturday afternoon/evening so any delayed flights, etc. would need to be communicated. I must have experienced hundreds of moments waiting at houses for renters whose mobile was not switched on, who had decided to go shopping at the supermarket, who were queuing for a hire car for two hours, whose flight had been delayed, whose train was stuck en route from Paris. I heard all the reasons under the sun why people arrived two to four hours late without contacting me which would cause me to rush across the countryside to try to avoid being late for people arriving at the next house. Oh, the joy of never having to wait for renters any more. At best all I could say to them was "I was expecting you at four o'clock" when they arrived at six thirty but, given they could sometimes have been travelling all day, it was difficult to protest or be unpleasant. Certainly, not the best way to start a holiday and a snarly welcome would surely be noted on one of the many feedback sites.

Coming a close second to kicking my heels and waiting for people, would be maggots and dustbins sitting in 35°+ heat. I included information about the dustbin collection day as part of walking the people around the house and garden. It was also mentioned in the A-Z house file with the need for everything to be in black plastic bags. Nevertheless, people would inevitably forget and I'd arrive on a Saturday morning with a rental due in the afternoon only to be greeted by an overflowing dustbin. Many people had ignored the need for refuse sacks and just thrown dirty nappies, chicken carcasses, and general mess straight into the bin. This could mean that the bin collectors could actually refuse to empty the bin in future which would affect the owners and future renters. In my desire for new arrivals to have a clean property, it meant I had no choice other than to empty the bin myself. I would always have a supply of rubbish sacks and it meant delving into the bin that was heaving with maggots that had multiplied in their hundreds in the heat. It was a revolting job and I would have to dump the bin bags in my car only for one or two maggots to go rogue and crawl around my boot. Another job that I was happy draw a line under.

There were definitely bonuses to offset the frustration of dustbin lice. This could be the amount of fruit and vegetables left at the end of a rental together with the occasional bottle of wine. I would often gain juicy melons, succulent peaches and nectarines, an array of courgettes, onions and tomatoes. I never needed to buy a garlic from June to September as I could rely on one being left. I always ensured a clean fridge but would leave any bottles of fresh milk or jars of preserves. From time to time, renters would delight in saying they'd left me food in the fridge which could be a bit Russian roulette in terms of what I would find. When you have a fish allergy, finding three quarters of a fish pie is not that appealing. Fortunately people catching a flight, and with rules and regulations on liquids, meant that a bottle of wine would often be sitting alongside that fish pie!

Some people rent out their houses and keys are collected from a neighbour and the tourists are then very much on their own. Although I can see the advantages in cost, most of the renters that I have dealt with have chosen a house for the reason that they are assured a welcome, an explanation of the property and a point of contact in case there are any issues. I am not party to any statistics but I suspect managed houses are chosen more regularly than a neighbour being a key holder.

Chapter 12
House Sales and Purchases

I've touched on the fact that I could be contacted to help with house sales or purchases. My time working for estate agents when I arrived in 2003 proved to be very useful. The knowledge that I had acquired, combined with second home owners not being available, meant that I was a natural choice to arrange estimations, manage viewings, and sometimes act as Power of Attorney. Often the owners or buyers were unable to attend one or both of the two meetings that were required: Le Compromis de Vente (*sales agreement*) and L'Acte de Vente (*sales act*).

I really enjoyed these transactions and they were the moments that were the closest to my U.K professional life before I became a Property Manager. A number of the notaires (*solicitors*) did not speak English so in some instances, I was the translator. I had to be attentive and educated in the process to ensure that my client was not duped in any way and equally not committed to anything that was not achievable. The contracts would include "Clauses Suspensives" (*conditional clauses for the sale*) and these were the conditions outside of the standard text and could apply to the buyer or the seller. It was not uncommon to see that a sale would only proceed subject to the diagnostic checks not identifying any major concerns. These were checks that tested for lead, asbestos, termites and the energy efficiency rating of the property.

There was one house sale that took a number of visits to a Land Registry to resolve. The house that had witnessed the burglary with the intruders attacking the son had been purchased about seven years previously and about three years before I started working for him. He had eventually decided to sell the house as it was not being used enough and maintenance issues were beginning to occur to which he did not want to commit his finances.

For some reason, when he bought the house, the addition of the swimming pool in the lower garden had never been acknowledged on any plans. This became a hurdle for the future sale although it did not appear to have prevented him from buying the house. I suspect the pool had not been noted on their sales document. The seller had in fact built the swimming pool without any authorisation. After a number of years of a construction, and with no objection from the neighbours, the addition has to be accepted as endorsed. Even so, the notaire was pushing for some form of approval. I had to go to the Trésor in Alès and to the equivalent of a Land Registry office. They had no documentation confirming the addition and it started to look a bit "iffy" with a possibility of the pool being removed and the land filled back in. I explained that the addition was not made by the current owner and it was a historical issue. In the end, and not without much huffing and puffing, they endorsed the change and eventually sent through a revised plan of the parcel of land.

I often found myself reassuring buyers or sellers of properties on the precision of flooding in the region. The rules had changed in France and it became law to identify all floodable towns and villages together with details on the level of impact. This could often be alarming when seen in print by a buyer, even if the house was located at the highest point in a village. I had to support the notaire in certain cases as my knowledge of the property location was detailed and I had often witnessed water flow when we experienced "les épisodes cévenols". These still occur and, in really intense episodes can hit 600mm, so it is easy to see why the notaires now have some obligation to define the problem areas. France is no different to England, Scotland or Wales in that land, previously noted as floodable, is now being used to build new housing estates. The consequences are all too evident to see at these times.

A memorable occasion during house-hunting was helping the son of an existing client. I had contacted the agencies and set up five meetings for properties that he wanted to visit. Having mostly looked at old stone houses in small villages, it was a shock to me that he opted to see a modern villa in one of the towns. I was driving him and his girlfriend around the various locations in my recently purchased and brand new Renault Clio so I had plenty of time to chat in between the viewings. He had an edgy manner and I wasn't enamoured with his attitude towards the agents. He was dismissive of anything he didn't like and made no attempt at pleasantries. We arrived at the villa where I parked up avoiding one of the many metal posts that France love to use on pavements. There was no sign of the agent and he immediately announced that the villa was too modern and he was not going to bother with the viewing and we could leave. By now the owner was in the garden to greet us so I explained that it was not protocol in France to pull out of a viewing with the owner at the gate waiting for us. I was privately thinking it would be rude in any country. I did my best to cajole him and explained it would at least be a comparison in price that could be useful in the future. Reluctantly, he agreed to honour the viewing. He trailed around the house showing zero interest and with me waxing lyrical on the seller's choice of colours, room size, etc.

Once back at the car, I got in and drove forward …..right onto the metal bollard I had forgotten was in front of me even if it was not visible!   It pushed the car upwards and then crunched back down with the bollard underneath. The front bumper and side panel were hanging off and water was running down the road. The situation got worse when the client said that the radiator could be split so I could not drive the 20 kilometres to my garage. I had to arrange a trailer to collect the car, rearrange our afternoon schedule and get them back to the hotel. I spent all day with them and was paid 240 euros. The car repairs came to 400 euros. Not happy, oh so very, very not happy!

Another frustrating occasion that springs to mind was when I was asked to offer advice on how to sell a property. It was a sweet house in the old quarter of a village and had a small roof terrace which adds significant interest as most people seek some form of exterior space here in the south where even the winters can be mild. The only negative was an open archway in the bedroom resulting in you being able to see through from the bedroom into the sitting room and vice versa. It was not to everyone's taste, however, it was still ideal as a first home for a young French couple or as a holiday home. I did quite a bit of work in advising the German clients who did not speak French but did speak a little English. I arranged two valuations and acted as interpreter and, just at the point it was to go on the market, the Maire stepped in and bought it for his daughter. All Maires have the right to know of property for sale in their community and are usually notified during the Notaire's searches. There was little that I could do about his decision even if I lost out on the resulting income from assisting the clients with future work. At least I got paid for the work that I had completed. Every year I was usually involved in a sale or a purchase – and sometimes both. These moments certainly helped my annual income.

For the most part, any client selling a holiday home would often find it was bought by someone also wanting it for the same reason. This meant that life continued as normal for me with just an amendment to the name on one of my many folders. The change of ownership would often be followed by a number of house restoration or house alteration projects so an increased workload was usually guaranteed.

Given the potential for a wide range of different cultures, it is important for a Property Manager to be diplomatic and never more so than when assisting with house sales or purchases. It is natural to have your client's interest at heart but the new buyers could equally become your new clients.

Chapter 13
Property Management Seasonal Routines, Occitanie

The summers are long and hot in the south and, if based in the Rhone valley, then you will know all about the Mistral wind that blows from the north plus the occasional Tramontane wind that blows from the north/north-west. Although weather forecasts can be helpful in predicting windy days, you can never totally understand when a Mistral might arrive. They delight in arriving at a moment's notice when you have left your house without securing the shutters or you've left laundry drying in the garden. It is rarer in the summer months, however, the winter and spring months are often the vulnerable times.

At its worst, I have seen empty dustbins picked up by the wind and hurled into the streets in front of passing cars. I've even had a dustbin land on my windscreen whilst driving. When it blows at 120 kmph, you don't really feel like driving or going outside as everything becomes a bit "Wacky Races" as you try to anticipate a falling branch from a tree, a dustbin, a scurrying villager wrapped in heavy overcoat with a woolly hat pulled down over their eyes.

Although it usually only blows for a couple of days, it can sometimes blow for more than a week and it's no surprise that they say you can become a little crazy after a few days. The constant tug-of-war happening outside your house is relentless and you do feel rather unhinged. Of course, with everything bad usually comes something good and this is the case with the Mistral. It's the reason we have such pure air as no pollution settles in this region. It also provides a spectacular light which has attracted so many artists to this corner of the world. When it blows, we complain and we moan. All the benefits it brings seem hard to bring to mind and yet there is the refrain in the Mistral song that reminds us:

V'là l'bon vent, v'là l'joli vent
V'là l'bon vent ma mie m'appelle
V'là l'bon vent, v'là l'joli vent
V'là l'bon vent ma mie m'attend

The seasons are well marked as I have mentioned before. You only need to walk into a local supermarket to know which month prevails. What grows on the land, appears in the shops. We can get cold snaps and occasional frosts, however, mostly the winter months pass quickly and it is usually very memorable if we ever see snow. In 17 years, I have seen it twice. Once, it landed but disappeared within an hour as the ground was too warm, the other occasion was less brisk and it settled and froze creating a hazard throughout the village until local farmers eventually cleared the roads.

You learn to wax and wane with the months that, even with climate change, tend to have a structure to them year on year. You might hear the occasional chuntering of "ce n'est pas normale" (*it's not normal*) when the climate advances crops by a couple of weeks yet month on month, we can usually anticipate the barometer.

With this in mind, I have outlined an idea of the additional duties besides checking over a house and garden/courtyard as this extra vigilance varies across the seasons. It will also vary if you are in a different region of France or based elsewhere.

Some people asked me what I looked for when I did house checks and garden checks. Now that I no longer have the business, a number of clients have found their new Property Manager a comfort but not a problem solver and this was the added value that I always offered. When a problem was identified, I would always contact the owners and would offer solutions; many of which I then had to follow up and take the necessary actions. It seemed logical to me and an intrinsic part of the role. It is clear that some people prefer to indicate a problem but then step away from any ownership until it's fixed. I see that as a potential loss of revenue even if the problems could sometimes cause sleepless nights.

The house inspections would start from the moment that I arrived at the front door or the gate. I would look for any abnormalities whilst also emptying the letterbox. Given France's affinity with weekly junk mail and its potential in declaring an unoccupied house, I always ensured there was a sign on every letterbox clearly noting "Pas de Pub". These were available for purchase in any decent hardware store.

If you have properties with electronic gates, you will always need the key to manually open them if there is a power cut or the clients prefer the electricity off during their absence. I had numerous occasions when an override key was required for electric gates. I would then normally walk the garden looking for any changes to the trees, fences, hedges, etc. Sometimes a neighbour would see me and ask me to contact the owners about overhanging branches that would need to be cut back. I also checked if there were signs of the gardener having visited and would chivvy them up if the exterior was looking neglected. I checked any sheds or pool rooms as part of the exterior process.

On entering the house, I would walk through each room. Again, it was a case of listening and looking. Every house has its own set of foibles. I have loads in my 19th century stone house. I know its weaknesses and strengths. You need a good set of antennae that can determine if something has changed within a room plus a good set of ears and eyes to hear water from split pipes (advisable to always disconnect water) or see traces of rodents. As and when clients were arriving, I would verify if the cleaner had visited and if the house was in order. Some houses would never change and others seem to attract issues like magnets. It was usually related to the age of the property or the level of upkeep by the owners. Sometimes a small one bedroomed, poorly maintained house could cause many more issues than a six bedroomed mansion.

If you are looking after old stone houses then there is always the possibility of damp. Some people put in dehumidifiers, however, these need the water reservoir to be emptied very regularly. An alternative concept is the "galets" or tablets that you can buy that come with a small box as a start-up unit. You put one of the large tablets in the box and they absorb the moisture in the air and tend to reduce odours of mustiness. This is an activity that is all year round so I have not shown it in the monthly list. The suppliers suggest a tablet lasts up to 3 months in a room that is approximately 20m² but my experience has found that this is not always the case. The tablets can be purchased in supermarkets and D.I.Y. stores.

Chapter 14
Closing the Business

A few months before I eventually wound up the business, I realised that I was becoming bored by the routine. I have never been one to cut corners or do a half-hearted job so I did not want this lack of enthusiasm to have a negative effect on my duties nor my clients. It had been a great job for fifteen years and I loved working for myself and having control over my diary. I had met so many people, experienced so many cultures, looked after a range of properties from a restored, one bedroom village house through to a majestic chateau in a vast park.

To close the business proved very easy; a real walk in the park compared to setting it up. I gathered up the necessary paperwork and headed to the CCI (Chambre de Commerce et d'Industrie) in Nîmes. I had to complete a form at the Reception desk and I left it with them. It was not necessary to have a meeting, provide a reason, or have any other interaction. The Reception desk personnel confirmed that I would receive official notification within a couple of weeks. This proved to be the case when I received an "Attestation de Radiation".

URSSAF, an organisation which manages the business subscriptions, contacted me to know the closing revenue for the year so they could assess any contributions that might be outstanding. I paid monthly direct debits but each year had a variable revenue so I always had tweaks in the last two months of the year's payments; mostly owing money and not being reimbursed. The only area that was unsettling was in the final adjustments of the subscriptions. One minute I had a letter saying I was to be reimbursed 447 euros, only in the same post to get a letter saying I owed them 391 euros. It went on like this for a number of communications until they eventually decided I owed them 256 euros. Any advance or rien ne va plus (*no more bets*)?

Some months after the closure, I received a new Kbis which noted the "radiation" (de-listing) of the business. I had gone full circle.

If the role of Property Manager appeals to you, it will provide many moments of friendship, surprise, laughter and dismay in equal proportions, and stories that you will "dine out on" for years. Those who are successful are good communicators, considerate of others, have a good command of software tools such as Excel and Word, and a natural ability in problem solving. It would be a good idea, if you are thinking of doing this role full-time, to ensure that you combine the job with another source of income such as house rentals where rental commissions will help boost your income and carry you through the quieter months.

Although the role in America is more closely aligned to managing tenants and rental contracts for a property owner, it is a much wider brief for someone who looks after holiday homes and I am certain it's much more rewarding and varied. Naturally, there can be distressing times like a fire or a break-in and yet, interwoven between any major event, you will have uncomplicated months of house checks and liaising with workmen. Times where you delight in being your own boss and managing your own diary which is such a godsend if you have spent years being constrained by office politics and "big business". I cannot guarantee there won't be sleepless nights tossing and turning about a client's house or a chewy problem but, for the most part, those times are rare and a reflection of your personality so perhaps not everyone will adopt such a level of responsibility.

It seems a very long time ago that I was sitting on that plane and suggesting to the British couple that I could help them find their permanent home in France. It is not without a sense of pride that I look back on creating and building a business in a foreign country and all that it entailed. There is no better feeling than winning a contract and adding a new client to your portfolio. It took me a while to develop some of the marketing tools to help promote my name in the region even though there is no doubt that clients spawned clients. It was an infrastructure of word of mouth which is totally understandable given the role.

I hope that you will benefit from my experience and it will encourage you to work abroad, be a Property Manager, or create your own company. Even without the business binding the relationships, I still have many clients who invite me to their homes for a meal or an aperitif even though the business no longer exists. The role of Property Manager continues to reward.

Appendices
Business Tools and Documents

A. Example of a Kbis
B. Client contract
C. Keyholder contract
D. Example of a task sheet and cash float management
E. Managing fire, flood and theft
F. Introductory email to assess a house for rental
G. Costs to rent your home
H. Property rental checklist
I. Rental contract
J. A-Z house folder
K. Seasonal additions to house checks

A.Example of A Kbis (information has been deleted to deter identity theft)

Extrait du registre du commerce et des sociétés

IMMATRICULATION ET IDENTITE DE LA PERSONNE

numéro d'immatriculation :   ' RCS Nîmes

date d'immatriculation :   12 octobre 2006

état civil :   **MEREDITH Gillian Anne**

     né(e) le :   ' - Royaume-Uni - de nationalité britannique

     Nom d'usage : Mademoiselle MEREDITH Gillian

     domicilié(e) :   - FRANCE

situation matrimoniale :   célibataire

CARACTERISTIQUES DE L' ENTREPRISE

activités principales de l'entreprise :   Prestation de services pour particuliers propriétaires de résidences secondaires : contrôle des résidences, entretien courant, jardinnage, accueil des visiteurs, suivi administratif de gestion courante. Mise en relation d'acheteurs étrangers avec des agences immobilieres de la région.

nom commercial :   il n'est pas déclaré de nom commercial

ETABLISSEMENT PRINCIPAL

adresse :

activité exercée :   l'activité exercée dans cet établissement est identique aux principales activités de l'entreprise

date de début d'activité :   01 novembre 2006

origine :   création

mode d'exploitation :   exploitation directe

MENTIONS ET OBSERVATIONS

néant

Toute modification ou falsification du présent extrait expose à des poursuites pénales.
Seul le greffier est légalement habilité à délivrer des extraits signés en original,
toute reproduction du présent extrait même certifiée conforme est sans valeur.

Pour extrait certifié conforme

DELIVRE à Nîmes le 12/10/2006

Le greffier

B.Suggestion for a Client Contract

Here's an example of what I put in place for my standard contract which included all aspects of the business:

THIS AGREEMENT is made the .... day of .... 20xx BETWEEN (your name) residing at (your address), and (client name) of (home address) in which (your name) will provide the selected services for the property situated at (address):

SERVICE A :
PROPERTY MANAGEMENT
Fee: ? euros per hour (plus mileage)
* *Key holder.*
* *Property security and maintenance checks.*
* *Empty letterbox, scan and email post as required, clear publicity material.*
* *Liaise with the Mairie (town hall) on your behalf.*
* *General administration e.g. liaise with internet provider, utility providers, etc.*
* *Arrange and oversee maintenance repairs.*
* *Project manage building renovations.*
* *Arrange and oversee deliveries, e.g. oil, wood, equipment, etc.*
* *Activate and deactivate automatic watering systems. Water pots.*
* *Open windows/doors to air the house prior to visits.*
* *Make up the beds before arrival.*
* *Switch on the fridge and stock with basics.*
* *Explain the house and facilities to friends using the property.*
* *Laundry following a house visit.*

AIRPORT/TGV PICK UP OR DROP OFF
* *List airports.*
* *List train stations.*

INTERPRETER
* *Act as interpreter.*

☐ *We require some of the activities in Service "A" as described above and may require*
   assistance in activities not noted in the above list.
☐ *We do NOT need Service "A"*

SERVICE B:
HOUSE SEARCH/HOUSE PURCHASE/HOUSE SALE
Fee: ? euros per hour (plus mileage)

- Liaise with estate agents and arrange viewings.
- View houses on your behalf. Provide independent assessment against your criteria
  to eliminate/reduce travel, hotel costs and time.
- Assist with notaire (solicitor) meetings and administration requirements.

HOUSE SALE
Fee: information on demand

- Point of contact for estate agencies. Open and prepare house in advance of agency visits.
- Point of contact for a private sale. Open and prepare the house and conduct visits.
- Point of contact between the clients and the owner and also with the solicitor.

☐ We require some of the activities in Service "B" as described above and may
   require assistance in activities not noted in the above list.
☐ We do NOT need Service "B"

SERVICE C :
RENTALS
CREATE HOUSE ADVERT ON HOLIDAY RENTAL WEB SITE
Fee: ? euros – site of choice or as per recommendation

- Take photos of house and resize for web based format
- Create description of property
- Create additional text explaining area and facilities
- Load house data onto web site
- Set up on-line rental availability calendar
- Set up tariff charges according to low/high season
- Load any supplementary charges e.g. electricity
- Create Booking Form
- Check beta version of site with clients and agree/modify as necessary
- Liaise with web site company on payment.

- Send subscription payment to rental site. (**Please note** this is a direct payment by the client and not included in the charge payable to your name.)
- Confirm with client when website advert activated.

☐ We require Service "C" as described above
☐ We do NOT need Service "C"

SERVICE D:
MANAGEMENT RENTAL ENQUIRIES AND BOOKINGS ON WEB SITE
Fee: ? % rental value of each booking
- Respond to enquiries and furnish information. No charge for information provided not leading to a booking
- Manage bookings and payment administration
- Collect booking deposit
- Collect balance
- Verify payments cleared before rental period starts
- Liaise with owner's appointed "meet and greet" representative
- Liaise with owner's appointed cleaner

☐ We require Service "D" as described above
☐ We do NOT need Service "D"

SERVICE E :
RENTAL POINT OF CONTACT AND MAINTENANCE MANAGEMENT
Fee: ? euros per hour (plus mileage if requested)

- Act as point of contact for renters
- Represent the owner in the event of any complaints or concerns
- Arrange artisans to carry out emergency repairs during rental period e.g. plumbing or electrical works

☐ We require Service "E" as described above
☐ We do NOT need Service "E"

SERVICE F :
A-Z HOUSE GUIDE AND PRACTICAL INFORMATION
Fee: ? euros

- Supply a ring binder
- Create a house guide (in English and in French) to help renters during their vacation
- Produce a list of practical information of the village/town and the region
- Supply a selection of leaflets of tourist attractions in the area
- Put all documentation in plastic protective wallets in order it remains clean

☐ We require Service "F" as described above
☐ We do NOT need Service "F"

TERMS AND CONDITIONS:

It is agreed that (your name) cannot be held responsible or liable for any damage to the property during the owner's absence e.g. flood, fire, theft.

It is agreed that (your name) cannot be held responsible or liable for any accident or injury to anyone at the property during the absence of the owner or during their occupancy of the house.

The agreement described and the services confirmed are agreed and signed by:

CLIENT SIGNATURE:

DATE:
Please hand write "Lu et approuvé" (read and approved) below your signature.

YOUR SIGNATURE:

C. Suggestion for a Keyholder Contract

THIS CONTRACT IS MADE ON (date) between (your name) living at (address) and (client name) living at (address) concerning the property situated at (holiday home address). (Your name) and (owner/s name) confirm that (your name) will supply the following services:

- Key holder of the property situated at (address) for the fee of xx € per month.

(Your name) cannot be held responsible for any situation which could occur during the period that the house is not occupied e.g. flood, fire, theft.

(Your name) cannot be held responsible for any accident or personal injury concerning the property when the house is occupied by the owners or any of their invited guests.

This contract, and services, has been read and approved by:

YOUR SIGNATURE:

CLIENT SIGNATURE(s):
Plus handwritten "lu et approuvé" if in France

DATE:

PLACE OF SIGNATURE:

D. Example of activity invoice and cash float management

date (winter)	weekly property check: lower radiators to frost setting, switch off hot water tank, ensure mains water off, flush toilets to avoid calcium build up. Check over house, pool room and shed. Empty letterbox. Forward mail to clients as instructed, send email to check if I need to open and scan a letter from Mairie.	? €
date (summer)	weekly property check: Disconnect fuse of hot water tank. Ensure mains water on for automatic watering system. House and shed check. Clear leaves and dead flowers from surface of swimming pool. Clean skimmer baskets of dead leaves and insects. Check pressure level of sand cylinder in pool room. Do a backwash as too high. Top up water level in pool and put in new chlorine tablets. Check letterbox. Email owners regarding opening post.	? €

TOTAL

OPENING CASH FLOAT (add date received) 150.00 €
Photocopy of receipts attached for purchases.

purchase date	chlorine tablets for swimming pool	15.00 €
purchase date	stamps to forward post	5.00 €
purchase date	ant powder	5.20 €

BALANCE CASH FLOAT 124.80 €

E. MANAGING FIRE / FLOOD / THEFT

How do you convey such bad news as a fire, a flood or a break-in at a property? One of the best approaches is to consider yourself as the customer and imagine how you would feel to hear this news. You will know your client so you will know if they are the type that takes bad news stoically or if they go into a complete tail spin. You need to consider this before picking up the phone, connecting to a video conference, or sending an email.

1.   What is the best method to convey the information to your clients - phone, video conference or email? Time zones might affect your choice.

2.   Outline exactly what has happened and take plenty of photos – or a video if possible.

3.   Take responsibility of the problem by arranging an appointment with the insurance assessor so the owner can see you have taken charge. For break-ins, check what steps you can take immediately to secure the property.

4.   Preserve the scene so the insurance assessor sees exactly what happened. Do not move anything without taking a photo of the original scene and have good reasons why anything has been moved/adjusted.

5.   Ensure regular ongoing communication between you and the client. A face to face video call can be more reassuring than emails in which there are risks that words can be misconstrued.

6.   Ensure you understand your level of responsibility in helping restore the property.

7.   Once the insurance assessor has visited, there are two possibilities for the repair of the

property. The insurance company may have specialists they use and who they can propose or you will need to draw upon artisans who have worked at the house previously. Identify which system is available.

8. Once the artisans involved in the repair have seen the damage, provided quotes that have been agreed by the owners (check if the insurer needs to see them), then I suggest you draw up a project plan. If you already have Project Management experience then this will be a skill in your toolbox but it is not hard to implement a basic system. Using Excel, list down every step required to get the house back into order; this might be breaking it down per workman e.g. builder, electrician, plumber. Put in an estimated start date and a completion date for each action and use a traffic light system of RED (action not started), AMBER (action pending or reliant on a previous task) GREEN (action completed). This will help you know your progress at a glance and be invaluable for the clients.

9. Verify how the insurer wants to receive the invoices. Do they want to receive them as they arrive or grouped together at the end of the work? Check if they will pay them directly to the renovator/artisan or if the client has the initial responsibility to pay them and will then be reimbursed.

10. COMMUNICATION, COMMUNICATION!

F. Suggested Introductory email to assess a house for rental

Hello Mr/Mrs .... (or Christian name if you you've spoken on the phone and feel it is more cordial).

Please find a draft contract attached which indicates my fee to create a rental advert for your property on an international holiday rental web site together with costs to manage the administration process.

Alternatively, I can meet you at your house to offer advice. Owing to the time that it would take to cover all relevant areas, my charge would be xx euros. This would be fully refundable in the event I am engaged to manage your house rental and that there is a signed contract.

The meeting would cover the following areas plus wider discussion:

- *Offer advice on effective web sites*
- *Discuss the terms and conditions for renting e.g. would you accept young children, smoking inside the property, pets? Offer advice based on 15 years' experience.*
- *Advise on the owner's responsibilities*
- *Advise on the renter's responsibilities*
- *Provide suggested weekly rates for your property with seasonal variances*
- *Identify and discuss potential supplementary charges*
- *Provide a list of costs to help you calculate if renting your house would be cost effective*

Please do not hesitate to contact me should you wish to arrange an appointment.
Regards
(name and mobile phone number)

G.An example of costs to rent your home

Here is an idea of what to consider if you want to rent a holiday home:

- *Web site fee to advertise the property as a holiday rental (an annual subscription fee or a pay-per-reservation fee).*

- *Commission to the person managing rental enquiries and bookings (usually between 10 – 15% of booking value).*

- *Check in of renters. (Always someone suitably customer focused who can manage issues such as breakdown of hot water tank, noisy neighbours or neighbour complaints by renters, tripping fuse boxes, etc.)*

- *Check out of renters and return of damage deposit.*

- *Cleaner.*

- *Laundry charges.*

- *Tourist Tax.*

- *Installation of WIFI internet access.*

- *House maintenance.*

- *Garden maintenance.*

- *Pool maintenance.*

- *Utility costs: electricity, water, mains or bottled gas.*

- *Good network of artisans for emergency breakdown repairs.*

H. My Property Rental Checklist

PROPERTY RENTAL CHECKLIST:	
Surname/Christian Name	
Address	
Land line	
Mobile	
Email	
Skype	
Date house built	
Maximum number of house occupancy	
m2 living area of house accessible by renters?	
Children accepted?	
Baby equipment available in property?	
Smokers accepted?	
Pets accepted?	
Suitable for elderly? Number of steps to access house? Staircases?	
Wheelchair access?	
Separate kitchen or American kitchen/diner?	
Dining table seats how many?	
How many bedrooms?	
Size of beds	
Air conditioning or fans in bedrooms?	
Number of bathrooms/shower rooms equipment: baths, showers, washbasins, bidets, separate toilets	
Method of heating off season?	
Smoke detectors fitted? (legal requirement)	
House fitted with alarm? Do renters have to set it during their rental period?	
Telephone line access?	
Internet access? Wifi?	
TV? Any international channels?	
DVD?	

Facilities: dishwasher washing machine machine clothes dryer or freestanding rail? coffee percolator toaster iron/ironing board electric oven or gas electric or gas hob unit fridge with ice box or fridge and freezer combo? microwave electric kettle	

EXTERIOR

m2 of garden/courtyard/terrace	
Orientation of garden and/or terraces	
Swimming pool	
Size of swimming pool and orientation	
Type of filtration (e.g. sand with chlorine galet?)	
Pool security – alarm, roller shutter and/or fence	
Jacuzzi	
Sauna	
Pool sun loungers available - how many	
Sun parasol(s)	
Barbecue - gas or coals	
Bicycles available for rental	
Car parking and how many vehicles	

FINANCIALS

Rental price low season (October - May)	
Rental price mid season (June and Sept)	
Rental price high season (July and August)	
Linen charge included or supplementary charge?	
Post rental cleaning included or supplementary charge?	
Taxe de Séjour payment?	
Reservation payment in full or two part payment?	
How much security deposit?	

Credit cards accepted with surcharge?	
Top 10 inventory checks on check-out day	

MISC

Dates to note "unavailable" when owners at house	
Distances: airport station motorway	
nearest bakery, shops, supermarket, bank, post office	
Restaurants	
Pharmacy	
Doctor	
Golf	
Tennis	
Name to be given to property e.g. "L'Ancienne Epicerie"	

Any other notes :

I.What to include in a Rental Contract

What to include in your rental contract:

Owners name together with the address of the rental home.

Request contact details of main rental contact and name of other renters (including age of any children).

Confirm dates of rental and number of nights at property.

Earliest check in time and latest check out time.

Charges outside of rental fee paid to web site (e.g. bedding, electricity).

Cancellation policy (undoubtedly on web site but always good to reinforce).

"On day of arrival" paragraph if you are expecting to be paid for bedding/towels or prefer a cash damage deposit rather than one controlled via a web site.

Terms and Conditions of the rental: maximum number of people, whether a pet is allowed, renter responsibility for use of pool, etc. Add anything that you feel best protects your house and any accident or injury to a renter.

Suggested clause to cover the swimming pool:

Signature and date box. (Do not forget to add that they should write "lu et approuvé" below the signature even if contract is in English.

J.Topics to include in the A-Z House Folder

If creating an A-Z house file, here are some topics to consider and in most cases it is the location of the nearest one to the rental house together with opening hours. It is certainly useful to point out if there is a specific day a shop, such as a bakery, is shut.

Bakery
Banks including nearest cash point
Butcher
Bicycle Rental
Dentist
Doctor
Dustbin and Recycling
Emergency numbers: Police, Fire, Medical, Embassy
Location in house of fuse box
Location in house to cut off mains water
Internet network name and password
Point of contact during a rental for any house/pool/garden problems
Markets – tourists understandably love the outdoor markets across France
Petrol Station
Post Office
Restaurants (recommendations always sought)
Security (the obvious areas plus add any metrological variances such as the Mistral wind in the South of France)
Sightseeing – include pamphlets of local tourist attractions
Supermarkets including any open on a Sunday morning
Taxi companies
Tourist Information Office

K. Seasonal Additions to the House Checks

January:
Check for wind damage (e.g. aerials, roofs, fences).
Ensure mains water off (particularly if a property is being cleaned periodically).
Ensure water drainage traps are clear of detritus.

February:
Ensure clients have lavender/pine anti-mite deterrents in their wardrobes.
Check for wind damage (e.g. aerials, roofs, fences).
Ensure mains water off (particularly if a property is being cleaned periodically).
Ensure rain water drainage traps are clear of detritus.

March:
Ensure mains water off (particularly if a property is being cleaned periodically).
Weeding and gardening if prepping house for owner arrival at Easter.

April:
Arrange appointment for swimming pools to be opened early May.
Check automatic watering systems for:
- breaks in pipework
- automatic watering jets for lawn mower damage and accuracy of water direction
- gout-à-gout rubber tube systems – check for split tubes/lost watering heads
- replace batteries to ensure supply during power outages

May:
Program automatic watering systems.
Ensure swimming pool maintenance issues resolved and pool opened for season.
Some ad hoc watering if required as temperatures can be 23+ towards end of month.
Arrange chimneys to be swept (often cheaper during the summer months). Some house insurance contracts insist this is done annually.

June/July/August:
Adjust automatic watering systems as necessary.

ACKNOWLEDGEMENTS

My thanks to all my clients over the years. So many became good friends. We laughed at the good times and drowned our sorrows with a few glasses of rosé during the bad times.

My thanks to the clients who encouraged me to write down my story. I only wish I'd kept a notebook to jot down all the crazy times when I wondered what the heck I was doing as there must be many "stories" left untold in this book.

I wish all future and current Property Managers every success. It is a great job which will provide many interesting challenges and, who knows, maybe you will find yourself writing a book as a result? Make sure to note down those mad moments as it might be hard to remember them after many years.

Bonne chance!
Gill

Sometimes being a Property Manager can feel like pushing water up hill. At times like this, I reflect on the time I asked my clients for a reference when I thought I might return to the U.K. Here are some examples that make my heart sing:

Gill has been our property manager for ten years now, since being recommended by a mutual friend. Her services have been invaluable. She cares for the good upkeep and condition of our house as if it were her own -- which is so reassuring, given that we're an 8-hour flight away. She ensures everything stays in mint condition and is exceedingly respectful of our property as a whole. Gill also handles our rental web site, books and manages clients, deals with tradesmen, translates documents and handles innumerable other management details. We've found her to be exceptionally reliable, competent, honest and a pleasure to work with. Her French skills are excellent. Truly not sure what we'd do without her

Sometimes being a Property Manager can feel like pushing water up hill. At times like this, I reflect on the time I asked my clients for a reference when I thought I might return to the U.K. Here are some examples that make my heart sing:

Gill has looked after our house in Uzès since we bought it. We live in Australia and cannot imagine how we could manage to maintain and rent out a house in France without Gill. Her efficiency was particularly evident when our house was flooded and she dealt with insurance assessors and numerous tradesmen to get the house back into a habitable state in an amazingly short time. She is capable, extremely professional and a mine of information and good advice. We could not recommend Gill highly enough to anyone looking for someone to manage their house in France.

Sometimes being a Property Manager can feel like pushing water up hill. At times like this, I reflect on the time I asked my clients for a reference when I thought I might return to the U.K. Here are some examples that make my heart sing:

I have known Gill Meredith for at least fifteen years. During that period she has been the key holder for my house in the south of France. She is conscientious and thorough and totally honest. Although living in a small village, she is absolutely discreet. She is also computer and tablet, etc. competent. She handles various difficulties with infinite patience and success.

She has on numerous occasions looked after my cat when I have been absent for short periods. This involved her coming to the house at least three times a day, to feed her, let her into the garden and spending time with her during my absence. My cat, as is often the case with cats, can be stand-offish with people. But Gill's affection and care won her over and they have become firm friends. I would never hesitate to leave any domestic animal in her care.

I can highly recommend Gill in every aspect of home and animal care.

Sometimes being a Property Manager can feel like pushing water up hill. At times like this, I reflect on the time I asked my clients for a reference when I thought I might return to the U.K. Here are some examples that make my heart sing:

For seven years, Gill Meredith has provided us with a broad range of services in our residence in France. She has done so effectively and with constant good humour. Initially a secondary residence, Gill managed our seasonal rentals i.e. directed the administrative management of contracts, payment, managed the checking in and out of tenants and the maintenance/care between rentals.

Sometimes being a Property Manager can feel like pushing water up hill. At times like this, I reflect on the time I asked my clients for a reference when I thought I might return to the U.K. Here are some examples which make my heart sing:

Gill has worked with us regularly over the past year and it has been wonderfully reassuring to know that our property has been in safe, competent hands while we have been away. She has proved to be professional, utterly reliable, discreet and resourceful. She has such green fingers that our plants have thrived in her care and she seems to have a benign influence on pets also. We recommend her without reservation.

Sometimes being a Property Manager can feel like pushing water up hill. At times like this, I reflect on the time I asked my clients for a reference when I thought I might return to the U.K. Here are some examples that make my heart sing:

Since the house became our main residence, Gill continues to ensure regular monitoring during our absence: post mail management and administrative handling of emergencies, monitoring ad hoc maintenance work, occasional maintenance of the garden.

Gill has always proven to be very highly reliable. Her rigorous organization allows immense flexibility in dealing rapidly and efficiently with all sorts of situations.

Sometimes being a Property Manager can feel like pushing water up hill. At times like this, I reflect on the time I asked my clients for a reference when I thought I might return to the U.K. Here are some examples that make my heart sing:

Gill has looked after our property for eight years, which was a new build and inevitably gave rise to quite a number of teething problems. Without her help and advice, the whole task would have been much more difficult. She is proactive in sorting out any issues and totally reliable in continuing to look after the property for us. Because we are not able to visit the house as often as we would wish, we are comforted by the thought that everything is in safe and competent hands. It is a pleasure to deal with Gill and nothing ever seems to be too much trouble.

Sometimes being a Property Manager can feel like pushing water up hill. At times like this, I reflect on the time I asked my clients for a reference when I thought I might return to the U.K. Here are some examples that make my heart sing:

Gill Meredith has taken care of our holiday home since 2008 (periodic controls of the outside and inside of the house, letter box, etc.) Gill is very reliable and prudent. With her very skilled experience (also with technical equipment) she can often resolve any problem. Moreover, she knows a big network of professional artisans in the surrounding area and can engage their assistance and organises and keeps an eye on them when they are working at the house. Gill explains any actions by writing comprehensible and precise reports via email and text messages with photos where necessary. With Gill Meredith our holiday home is in good hands - without Gill we were missing "an angel".

Sometimes being a Property Manager can feel like pushing water up hill. At times like this, I reflect on the time I asked my clients for a reference when I thought I might return to the U.K. Here are some examples that make my heart sing:

When it came to looking after my house whenever I was away, Gill was indispensable: she regularly watered my plants, checked my mail, and made sure my house was secure at all times. Highly reliable, diligent, and trustworthy are just some of the many positive qualities that come to mind when I think of Gill Meredith. Gill was a godsend whenever I needed a cat sitter. A lover of cats herself, she took special care to ensure that LouLou was well-fed and happy, and if I needed her to, she could even administer cat medicine!! She also played with my cats, so they wouldn't feel lonely. I recommend her as a Property Manager without any hesitation.

Sometimes being a Property Manager can feel like pushing water up hill. At times like this, I reflect on the time I asked my clients for a reference when I thought I might return to the U.K. Here are some examples which make my heart sing:

We have known Gill for over 10 years. She was recommended to us by a friend in the U.K. We spend our time between the South of France and the U.K. We needed a Property Manager as we have two cats in France and we required a reliable person to homesit in our absence. She has proved to be not only reliable but also tidy, respectful, practical, totally discreet, and observant of any breakdown issues with the ability to deal with them. She is experienced, caring and attentive.
We had total peace of mind whenever we left our house and our cats in care.

BY THE SAME AUTHOR

MA CRÊPE SUZETTE : A LIFE IN FRANCE

A must read for anyone dreaming of moving to France and carving out a hassle free life. It opens with a leisurely introduction of how Gill became a Francophile, purchased a holiday home and decided to leave the power jobs behind her. The book covers the highs and lows of her Property Management business, her dealings with French bureaucrats and the joys of working in the South of France. This book will transport you to France where you will smell the wild rosemary, feel the Mistral wind and visualise the bright colours of the region. You can follow her transformation from quintessential business suit and high heels to shorts, polo shirt and espadrilles.

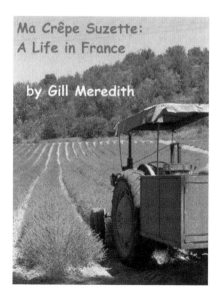

.... and coming soon:

"The Adventures of Lottie" by Gill Meredith

A recently widowed British woman discovers her husband's secret following many years of marriage. This secret leads her to the South of France where she throws away her old life and buys a brocante shop in Avignon and enters into the world of buying and selling antiques and bric a brac.

Before long Lottie finds herself caught up in a mystery in which she will encounter some very dubious characters. Whilst she is no weakling and has a gung-ho spirit, she has no idea of the danger that is around the corner.

Printed in Great Britain
by Amazon